Tabernacle Study Guide

Tabernacle Study Guide

Michael Ashton

The Christadelphian
404 Shaftmoor Lane, Hall Green, Birmingham B28 8SZ, UK

2022

First published 1989
Reset and reprinted 2022

ISBN 978 0 85189 127 9 (print edition)
ISBN 978 0 85189 422 5 (electronic edition)

Printed and bound in the UK by
CMP (UK) Limited

Contents

What is a Study Guide?

1. Aims: The overriding aim of all Bible study is that through knowledge and understanding of the word of God a person may become "wise unto salvation through faith which is in Christ Jesus" (2 Timothy 3:15, KJV).

   "Study Guides" are designed to explain the straightforward teachings of scripture and where appropriate to emphasise:

   a. First principles of doctrine

   b. Practical outcomes

   They should be helpful to young people, to those who are "young in the faith", who often have very little background knowledge of the scriptures, and to those of all ages and experience who enjoy straightforward, uncomplicated study of the Bible.

2. Other features of Study Guides

   a. Layout: After a brief introduction, the first study section ("A closer look") provides essential background information. "Finding your way" enables the reader to see an overall picture. Thereafter the study examines each item more closely. Headings and bold verse references make it easy to use the guide for looking up information on any section of the Bible text.

   b. Bible versions: This Guide mainly uses the New King James Version as a basis, as this helps to overcome problems of archaic expressions that exist in the Authorised (King James) Version (AV / KJV). Other versions can sometimes assist in clarifying a particular passage, but some popular modern versions are unreliable and betray the doctrinal bias of their translators.

   c. Manageable sections: Each Guide is divided into units of study which are not too long. This will make it easier for individuals or groups to make progress. An hour's concentrated and productive study on a regular basis is likely to yield good results.

   d. Visual help: The prophets and the Lord Jesus himself used visual illustrations to communicate their message. While the prime emphasis is on the written word, visual help is given wherever possible to increase understanding.

   e. Use alongside the Bible: The student must have a Bible open alongside the Guide. It is recommended at the outset that important information is marked in the Bible. Have a pencil at the ready.

   f. Assessment of Progress: At the end of each section you are invited to "Test yourself". Some questions ask for factual recall, others for understanding, others are open-ended, challenging readers to relate the lessons learned to their own lives. It is suggested that readers write down their responses before looking up the suggested answers supplied towards the end of the Guide. This ensures a good understanding has been achieved before moving on.

   g. Further Study: The final sections contain suggestions for further study and a recommended book list.

   h. Prayer: We are studying the word of God. Before commencing any Bible study we must ask God's blessing on our activity. Thank God for making the Bible available to us, so that through it we may come to know Him and to look forward to His coming kingdom.

Here is a prayer that sums up our aim:

"Open thou mine eyes, that I may behold wondrous things out of thy law."

(Psalm 119:18, KJV)

Preface

THE tabernacle has always been a source of interest to me, partly because of a one-time professional involvement in architecture, but primarily because it is able to show in a tangible form some of the abiding principles about salvation that God has laid down in His word.

In the tabernacle God provided a visual aid to help His people understand this process of salvation. Indeed, it is so wonderful a subject that all the various parts of the tabernacle are needed to open up the intricacies involved. When the details of the sacrifices and offerings, and the clothing of the priests and high priest are added, the amount of information regularly available to the God-fearing Israelite was very extensive and impressive. They could become quickly aware of God's mercy and grace, and discover more of His wonders as they meditated upon what was required from them in His service.

All Bible Study is like this. The basic framework of God's purpose can be grasped relatively easily. The youngest children can thrill to the message contained in its fascinating stories. Yet there has been no sinful individuals, however intelligent they may be, who have ever completely plumbed its depths. Like everything that is most satisfying, God's word reveals its mysteries only to those prepared to work at understanding them, and to meditate upon their true meaning.

Any Bible subject can be studied by individuals, or by groups combining to discuss different aspects. The tabernacle theme is particularly appropriate for group study, and it is hoped that this guide can assist in structuring such a study to the benefit of those participating. The intention has been to present the subject in small sections allowing short passages to be completed at one sitting. The questions at the end of each section, and the additional assignments at the end have been included to extend the study and the personal researches of the student.

Even though Israel had in the tabernacle a constant visual reminder of these eternal principles in their midst, they did not believe automatically, nor were they led to appreciate the necessity of the work of the Lord Jesus Christ. Many of them rejected the offer of life extended to them by God. It is fervently hoped that the readers of this short study will not be blind to these important truths, but will recognise how necessary it is to understand what God wishes from His people, and will attempt to approach Him as He has directed. God desires to dwell in every human heart, and has said that the sort of people who will respond to Him correctly are those who are "poor and of a contrite spirit and tremble at His word". Perhaps a consideration of this subject will evoke this response in us.

Michael Ashton
Cofton Hackett, Worcestershire
September 2022

Acknowledgements

For assistance in the production of illustrations, grateful thanks are extended to Stephen Ashton, Mark Norris and Paul Wasson.

Introduction

ACCORDING TO THE PATTERN

JACOB'S family, numbering seventy people, who left Canaan for Egypt to escape a time of severe famine, grew rapidly in only 200 years to be a nation of over two million people.[1] When they became a threat to the Egyptians they were used as slave labour to build magnificent cities and tombs. Only when they were severely oppressed did they turn to God, and cry to Him for help.

Led out of Egypt

His response was dramatic. Under a leader, Moses, who had chosen a hard life among his own people rather than an easy life in the Egyptian court, God led the children of Israel out of Egypt. The night they left, every Egyptian firstborn died, but the Israelites were kept safe and intact. Miraculously they passed safely through the Red Sea on dry ground, but the Egyptian soldiers who followed them were drowned.

The people of God

In this special way the Israelites became God's people, His firstborn (Exodus 4:22). He had saved them from death, and redeemed them (bought them back) from slavery. He was always to be at the centre of their lives. As they journeyed through the wilderness, God provided ways that could impress upon them this simple truth: *To serve God properly, He must be honoured and respected*.

It was not sufficient, however, just to tell them this. Through Moses God established laws to act as a constant reminder of His holiness. And, to provide a continual visual reminder He also gave Moses instructions to build a special tent which would be at the centre of their encampment, and the focus of their worship. Like the provision of the Lord Jesus Christ in New Testament times, this tent, better known as *the tabernacle*, was to teach them about:

1. The Lord God Himself;
2. God's desire to meet with men and women;
3. How to approach Him; and
4. What He requires from all who wish to serve Him.

1 Based on the figure of "about 600,000" men, excluding women and children; plus a "mixed multitude" who also wished to flee from Egypt (Exodus 12:37,38).

An educational model

In the letter to the Hebrews the tabernacle and its furnishings are described as "patterns of things in the heavens" (9:23). It must therefore be considered as an educational model, designed to explain divine concepts in ways man can understand. The Apostle Paul explained that "the law [of Moses] was our schoolmaster to bring us to Christ" (Galatians 3:24). The construction of God's tabernacle is one of the most important of these lessons from the Law of Moses.

Yet all the details of its construction are not recorded in ways that would make it possible today to build a replica. That is not what God wants, and nor is it even possible to be certain exactly how it was put together. There are almost as many suggestions as there have been people who have considered the problem. The same is true of all the structures mentioned in the Bible: the tabernacle, Solomon's temple, and the temple described in Ezekiel's prophecy all require further information before we can be certain exactly what they looked like.

In the case of the tabernacle, Moses had been shown a "pattern" when he was in Mount Sinai and God, through His angels, gave him the Law. Moses then was able to oversee the work, and knew how to interpret the directions he had been given.

Because there are parts we are uncertain about, any visual impression given by the illustrations in this book must not be relied upon, only insofar as they represent what we are clearly told in the Bible. Every representation of the tabernacle has to use some 'artist's licence'!

So we are not being shown in the tabernacle how to build one ourselves, but how to draw important lessons from God about ourselves and our responsibilities before Him.

What is true in the Old Testament on a national level, must under Christ be applied to individuals. In the tabernacle the Israelites were reminded dramatically of God's continuing presence among them, and of the life of holiness He demanded of them: "Be ye holy; for I am holy", was the message given to the nation through Moses (Leviticus 11:44, as quoted in 1 Peter 1:16).

The lesson for today

For individuals who now respond to the Gospel message the challenge is the same: to ensure:

1. That the God of Israel is at the centre of our lives, honoured in everything we do; and
2. That our lives should reflect the holiness we learn from a consideration of His purpose.

CHAPTER 01

A closer look

THE CAMP OF ISRAEL

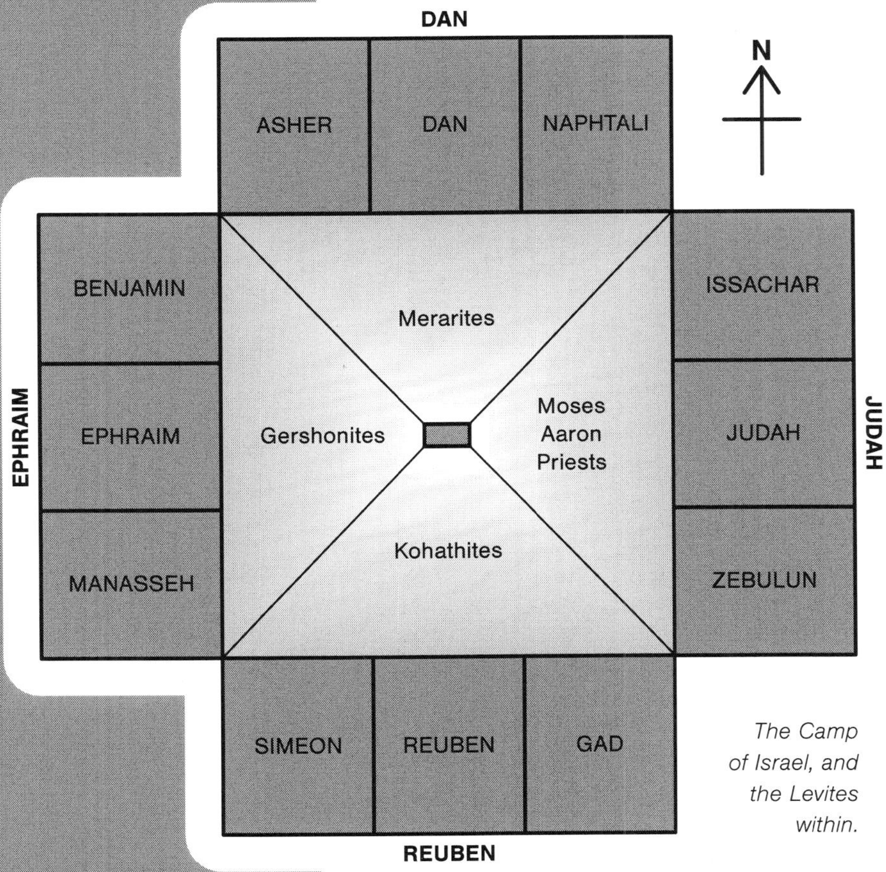

The Camp of Israel, and the Levites within.

THE organisation of a vast number of people in the wilderness would not be a simple task, and it required careful and efficient planning.

How it was organised

Because the people were all descended from the twelve sons of Jacob, it was possible to divide them into twelve groups, named after the twelve tribes. Both in the travelling arrangements through the desert and for their camps whenever they stopped, each tribe knew what they should do, and where they should position themselves.

The twelve tribes were even further organised into four groups of three, so that there were four leading tribes: Judah, Reuben, Ephraim, and Dan. The illustration shows how they camped, always in set positions; one to the north, one to the south, and the others on the east and west.

Because there was a special blessing on Joseph, two tribes were descended from him, named after his two sons Ephraim and Manasseh. This meant that there was a "thirteenth" tribe, the tribe of Levi, that was not in any of the four groups.

The tribe of Levi

Moses and his brother Aaron belonged to the tribe of Levi; it was to become the tribe of the priests. This had been implied when the name was first given to Jacob's son (Genesis 29:34): Levi means 'joined', and the function of the priests was to help bridge the gap between a Holy God and sinful man. The tribe of Levi had its own special place in the arrangements in the wilderness. When the nation was camped, the Levites' place was central among all the others. Like theirs, it was divided into four parts. Three were named after Levi's three sons, Gershon, Kohath, and Merari. The fourth part comprised Aaron's family, even though he himself was descended from Levi through Kohath. So, just as there were two tribes for Joseph in the main camp, there were two parts of the Levite's camp for Kohath.

Under the Law, the firstborn's share was always double that of the other sons. By this arrangement, even though they were not born first, Joseph and Kohath (Aaron) were treated by God as the firstborn. From what is recorded about these two men, we can deduce that God treated them this way because of their response to Him. God also chose the nation of Israel as His firstborn, even though it was a small and weak nation, not the first in anything, with little to recommend it:

> "But because the Lord loved you ... hath the Lord brought you out ... from the hand of Pharaoh king of Egypt." (Deuteronomy 7:8)

The High Priest

The proximity of the Levites to the tabernacle teaches another lesson. Even though Aaron and the High Priests who followed him were imperfect examples of the Lord Jesus Christ, the "great High Priest" to come, their placement always near the tabernacle, and Aaron's own tent immediately opposite the entrance to it, show that access to God can only be through the one He has appointed, who has merited that place by his own desire always to act in accordance with God's will.

God said the Levites were to camp by the tabernacle, "that there be no wrath upon the congregation of the children of Israel; and [they] shall keep charge of the tabernacle of the Testimony" (Numbers 1:53).

In the camp, Aaron's family had its place at the head of the section containing the tribes in Judah's group. The Kohathites were associated with Reuben's group of tribes; the Gershonites with Ephraim's; and the Merarites with Dan's.

All these arrangements formed a hollow square leaving a large area of clear ground in the centre of the national camp between a Holy God and a sinful people. This space was reserved for the tabernacle, and the faithful Israelite was intended to see a significant pattern in the foursquare arrangement, with God's tent in the middle – a pattern to assist him in his own life.

The breach between God and His covenant people had to be "bridged" before the process could be begin outside Israel with Gentile nations. Many men and women choose to live without acknowledging the importance of God, but His people were to have a continual reminder of His presence among them so that they would honour Him in everything they did.

On the march

When the nation was on the move, the arrangement was different. Instead of the tabernacle being at the centre of the multitude, its most important part spearheaded the travelling columns of people.

Right at the heart of the tabernacle was a simple rectangular box, known as the Ark of the Covenant. It was made of wood, but covered completely with gold. On it was placed the golden mercy seat, one of the most skilful pieces of craftsmanship ever produced. The Ark was not meant to represent God in the way heathen idols represented false gods, but it was intended to represent where God is pleased to dwell, as we shall see later.

The Ark was covered with a blue cloth for travelling, and was carried by the Kohathites leading the whole nation as they journeyed towards their next resting place.

The other parts of the tabernacle and its furnishings were separated into various groups and carefully distributed into special positions among the tribes. Thus, when the nation travelled, the "presence" of God was at their head, and the rest of His "house" (the tabernacle) formed an integral part of His people. See illustration on page 61.

This idea, of God always being at the centre and the head of His people, is emphasised time and again by the details of the tabernacle. Mankind had been separated from God by sin, but God conceived a wonderful and merciful plan by which the bond broken by sin could be restored. The tabernacle helps to explain this and also anticipates the time when God will be glorified in perfection. The ultimate completion of the purpose of God is described like this in the last book of the Bible:

> "Behold, the tabernacle of God is with men, and He will dwell with them, and they shall be His people. God Himself will be with them and be their God." (Revelation 21:3)

Leaving Egypt behind

When the Israelites left Egypt the Egyptians could not get rid of them quickly enough. Pharaoh changed his mind so often that only the death of the firstborn (particularly as this included his own son) could persuade him to let God's people go.

To encourage them to leave, the Egyptians pressed the Israelites to take all sorts of goods and precious jewels:

> "They asked [borrowed, KJV] from the Egyptians articles of silver, articles of gold, and clothing. And the LORD had given the

people favour in the sight of the Egyptians, so that they granted them what they requested. Thus they plundered the Egyptians."

(Exodus 12:35,36)

Though the people did not know it at the time, they were going to spend forty long years in the wilderness. All the adults, who received the precious things from the Egyptians, were going to die in the wilderness because of their lack of trust and confidence in the power and salvation of God. What good would the jewellery be to them in desert conditions?

They did not know that this also was a part of God's purpose, and one of the lessons He wishes to teach all people, not just those who were brought out of Egypt with Moses. In the Bible Egypt represents the world and the affairs of man, in contrast to Israel which represents the purpose of God.

The jewellery and precious stones were to be used as materials for the tabernacle. How else could they have obtained them when they were in the wilderness? God asked the people to give what they had, and it was those who were "willing hearted" who provided the things God's tent was made from (Exodus 25:2). Did you notice how this question was anticipated when the Egyptians gave them the jewels? The Israelites "borrowed" them! Nothing in this world belongs to us, for "the earth is the Lord's, and all its fullness" (Psalm 24:1). The things we have are given to us to see how we will use them.

The same choice is set before every generation: whether to satisfy self with the treasures of this world, or whether to devote them to the worship of God, and to use them in His service. This can involve possessions, houses, cars, or other goods; it can involve talents and abilities which when properly directed can bring honour to God's Name; but above all (and this is what was being shown by God's request to the Israelites), He requires wholehearted devotion. The call is to everyone to be "willing hearted".

The things of Egypt were going to be used to honour God's majesty, just as, when Christ returns, the world is going to have to learn God's ways, submit to His rule, and eventually reflect His glory. This is how the Bible describes that time:

"The kingdoms of this world have become the kingdoms of our Lord and of His Christ, and He shall reign forever and ever!"

(Revelation 11:15)

Let them make me a sanctuary

The Israelites could hardly have been unaware of the presence of God in their midst when they crossed the Red Sea on dry ground, or when He spoke to them from Mount Sinai. But as they moved away from that brooding mountain something else was needed to keep Him always in remembrance. There was, of course, the cloud which led them by day and appeared as a fiery pillar at night time. That was a visual indication

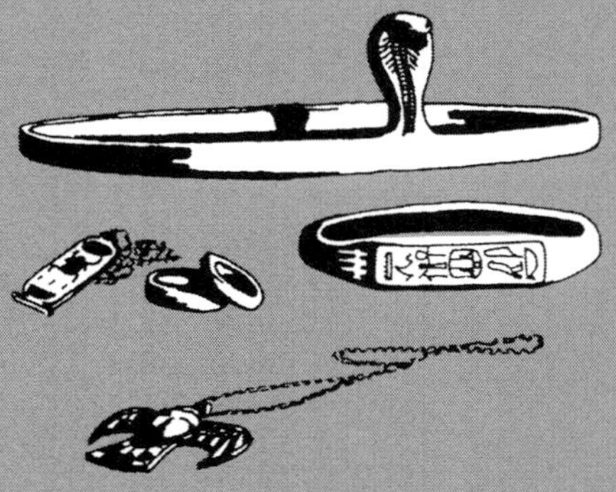

Egyptian jewellery

of the nearness of the angel of God's presence. During the long night when the Egyptian army was behind them and the Red Sea was in front, the cloud was their protection:

> "It was a cloud and darkness to the one [the Egyptians], and it gave light by night to the other [the Israelites], so that the one did not come near the other all that night."
> (Exodus 14:20)

The cloud showed the people where to go and when to camp:

> "Whenever the cloud was taken up ... the children of Israel would go onward in all their journeys. But if the cloud was not taken up, then they did not journey till the day that it was taken up." (Exodus 40:36,37)

This fiery cloud also showed the importance of the tabernacle, and that it was the place where God's presence would be seen in the centre of His people, for "the cloud covered the tabernacle of meeting, and the glory of the LORD filled the tabernacle" (Exodus 40:34).

It was thus "a sanctuary" (this word literally means 'a place set apart') specially for God. "Let them make me a sanctuary", God had said, "that I may dwell among them" (Exodus 25:8). By this means God was telling His people that He was *their* God and His comfort and protection would be with them so long as they honoured and trusted Him.

TEST YOURSELF

1. Where was the tabernacle sited in the Israelite camp?
2. Which tribe had its tents immediately next to the tabernacle?
3. Where did the materials come from to build the tabernacle?
4. What is a sanctuary?
5. How were the Israelites assured that the tabernacle was a sign of God's presence among them?
6. What was the function of the priests?
7. The tabernacle taught the Jewish nation. What lesson does it teach individuals today?
8. What possessions or abilities have you got that could be used in the service of God?

For answers turn to page 64.

The tabernacle and its parts

BEFORE looking in more detail at the construction of the tabernacle itself, and the purpose and positioning of its furniture, it will help if we can get an overall idea of its size and its various parts.

IT will possibly surprise us, having discovered that the tabernacle was the centre of worship for a nation the size of a very large modern city, to learn how small it was. The tabernacle 'building' itself measured only about 5 metres wide by 15 metres long (15 feet by 45 feet). As it was divided into two 'rooms', the larger one (5 metres by 10 metres) was not much larger than the living accommodation in a family house today!

The true meaning of worship

The answer to this apparent difficulty is that worship is commonly misunderstood. Mention the word to someone in the street and they will possibly think of a large cathedral, organ music and stained glass windows. Yet worship does not require large numbers of people and grand surroundings. Basically it is the response of each individual person to the God Who made all things. He does not ask men and women to think about Him only when they are in a crowd, or in a special building, but to glorify Him throughout their lives; in mundane, everyday tasks, *and* on important occasions; when times are good *and* when they are bad.

Who could go in?

Very few Israelites were allowed to enter the tabernacle. Only the priests (Aaron's family) could go into the larger 'room', and only Aaron himself as High Priest into the smaller one. Even then, he could only go in on one day each year, and only after he had made careful and special preparations!

The tabernacle was set in the centre of a courtyard, enclosed by a fence made from hanging curtains. Each Israelite was allowed to go to the entrance to this courtyard when making one of the offerings required under the Law of Moses. Apart from these occasions, the tabernacle, by a variety of means, was "set apart" from the people. It declared the holiness of God and, by contrast – because it could only be approached when bearing an offering for sin – it also declared the unworthiness of sinful man.

The outer court

The first part of the tabernacle, and the one seen by most people, was the outer court, about 50 metres long by 25 metres wide (150 feet by 75 feet). A standard-sized football pitch is

TEST YOURSELF

1. Under the Law, who was allowed to enter the tabernacle?
2. Approximately how large was the site reserved for the tabernacle?
3. What two items were placed in the court surrounding the tabernacle?
4. What were these two things used for?
5. Who was able to use them?

For answers turn to page 65.

exactly twice as long and twice as wide, so four tabernacle courts could fit on one football pitch! The court was formed from white curtains, with only one means of entry. This was a gateway, made with embroidered curtains.

Apart from the tabernacle itself, inside the Court were the following things:

- An altar; and
- A large basin.

These were both made from bronze (translated "brass" in the KJV), and were used in connection with the sacrifices.

The altar

This was 2.5 metres square and 1.5 metres high, hollow and with a grating inside it to support the fire and the sacrifice. Basically it was made from wood, but encased in bronze, and placed immediately inside the entrance to the courtyard.

In connection with the sacrifices, there were also various utensils: hooks, spoons, forks, etc., but no specific descriptions are given of these in the Bible.

The basin

Described in the NKJV as a *laver* (from the Latin *lavare*, meaning 'to wash'), this large basin held water used by the priests to wash themselves before *and after* they offered the sacrifices, or entered the tabernacle to serve. It was also made from bronze.

The tabernacle

The tabernacle itself had a highly ornate interior made from costly and precious materials using great craftsmanship, but with a drab and sombre exterior, made from dull coloured animal skins.

The inside was a wooden structure, completely covered with gold. Over this was placed a series of coverings – curtains of various kinds, all with different significances, but having the effect of carefully covering all the precious materials from sight, and cutting out natural light from the interior of the tabernacle.

The two 'rooms' in the tabernacle, separated by another curtain, called *The Veil*, were known as *The Holy Place* (the larger, and first room) and *The Most Holy* (or *Holiest*) *Place* (the second, smaller room).

The Holy Place

Priests entered this part of the tabernacle daily, to renew some of the offerings. Inside it were:

- The table of showbread;
- The lampstand; and
- The incense altar.

The Holy Place was entered through a doorway constructed from an exquisitely embroidered hanging curtain, and a similar one (The Veil) separated it from the Most Holy Place. The ceiling was formed from the first layer of tabernacle curtains, which were also embroidered. The walls were made from wood covered with gold.

Against all these rich and costly materials, the floor provided a stark contrast. It was the desert ground – a constant reminder of man's origins and certain destiny, for:

> "For dust you are, and to dust shall you return." (Genesis 3:19)

The table of showbread

One metre long, 50 cm wide and 75 cm high, the table for the showbread was made of wood covered with gold. It held twelve loaves of bread, representing the twelve tribes. These were replaced each week with bread from a fresh baking, and the old loaves were eaten by the priests.

The table stood to the right hand (north) side of the Holy Place.

The lampstand

The lampstand was made to support seven separate oil lamps which provided the illumination for the Holy Place. It was designed like a stylised tree, with a central trunk and spreading branches. A remarkable piece of workmanship, it was formed from *one piece* of gold carefully worked ("hammered") into the shape described by Moses after he had been shown a pattern by God.

The lamps were kept continually burning; the wicks needed regular trimming, and the oil had to be replenished. This was done twice a day, once in the morning and once in the evening.

The incense altar

In front of the veil which led to the Most Holy Place stood the Incense Altar. It was one metre high, and 50 cm square, again made from wood completely covered with gold. Incense was burnt on it, using hot coals from the main altar. The incense was specially made, so that when it was burnt it gave off a highly scented smoke.

The Most Holy Place

The dimensions of this room, 5 metres square, and 5 metres high, set in a building in the centre of an open square formed inside a huge square camp, show that here was the heart of God's sanctuary. There was nothing made by man which lighted this area. Like the holy city described in the Book of Revelation, it –

> "Had no need of the sun or of the moon to shine in it, for the glory of God illuminated it." (21:23)

The brightness of the glory of God, experienced by Moses when he received the Law on Mount Sinai, and which the Israelites could not bear to look at when they only saw the reflection still shining on Moses' face, was the light for the Most Holy Place. Although the light of God's glory would fill the whole room, there was a focal point from which it would shine.

The only furniture in the Most Holy Place was *The Ark of the Covenant* covered by the *Mercy Seat*. The glory of God shone from above the Mercy Seat, as if to show that this quality is the essence of God Himself. It was the way He described Himself to Moses:

> "The LORD, the LORD God, merciful and gracious, longsuffering, and abounding in goodness and truth, keeping mercy for thousands, forgiving iniquity and transgression and sin, by no means clearing the guilty." (Exodus 34:6,7)

The Ark of the Covenant

Sometimes called the Ark of the Testimony, this was a simple rectangular box, made from wood covered with gold. It was 1.25 metres long and 75 cm wide and high. It was named after what was stored inside it. The two stones inscribed with the Ten Commandments, God's Testimony of what He requires from man, and the basis of the covenant, were placed in the Ark as a constant reminder to Israel that on the day God spoke to them from Sinai they had said:

> "All that the LORD has said we will do, and be obedient." (Exodus 24:7)

These were not the only things in the ark. Here is the full list:

- The tables of the covenant;
- A golden pot containing some manna; and
- Aaron's rod that budded.

The Mercy Seat

On top of the Ark was a plate of solid gold, acting as a lid. As part of the lid and formed in one piece with it were two cherubs looking down onto the mercy seat and with their wings overshadowing it. The whole was to provide a throne for God:

> "Give ear, O Shepherd of Israel ... You who dwell between the cherubim, shine forth!" (Psalm 80:1)

TEST YOURSELF

1. What was surprising about the floor in the tabernacle?
2. What lesson should it have taught the Israelites?
3. What were the two areas in the tabernacle called?
4. What three items were placed in the first part of the tabernacle?
5. How were the two parts of the tabernacle lit?
6. What was kept in the Ark of the Testimony?
7. What covering was provided for the Ark?

For answers turn to page 65.

CHAPTER 02

Finding your way

INFORMATION about the tabernacle is contained in a number of places in the Bible. The following list sets out just the main passages in the book of Exodus connected with each separate part. Reference to the illustrations will help you get a picture in your mind of the different elements of the tabernacle structure and its furnishings. It will also help to read Exodus 25-27 and 35-38 through at least twice, before returning to this Guide.

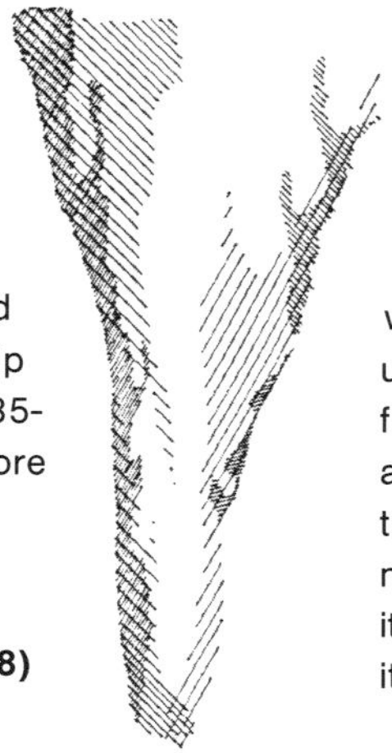

The purpose of the tabernacle (25:1-9; 40:34-38)

Though God has created all people on the face of the earth, He chose to reveal Himself through the nation of Israel. They would be silent witnesses to His existence and His abundant power. A correct appreciation of the tabernacle shows that the God of heaven chose to dwell on earth among His people and that it is still His desire to do so.

The materials and craftsmen (31:1-11; 35:4-35; 36:1-7; 38:21-31)

The materials for the tabernacle were donated willingly by the Israelites from the goods thrust upon them by the Egyptians when they escaped from slavery to Pharaoh. Two men, Bezaleel and Aholiab, were appointed by God to oversee the work. They were specially skilled in the necessary crafts to manufacture the various items of furniture – and the building itself.

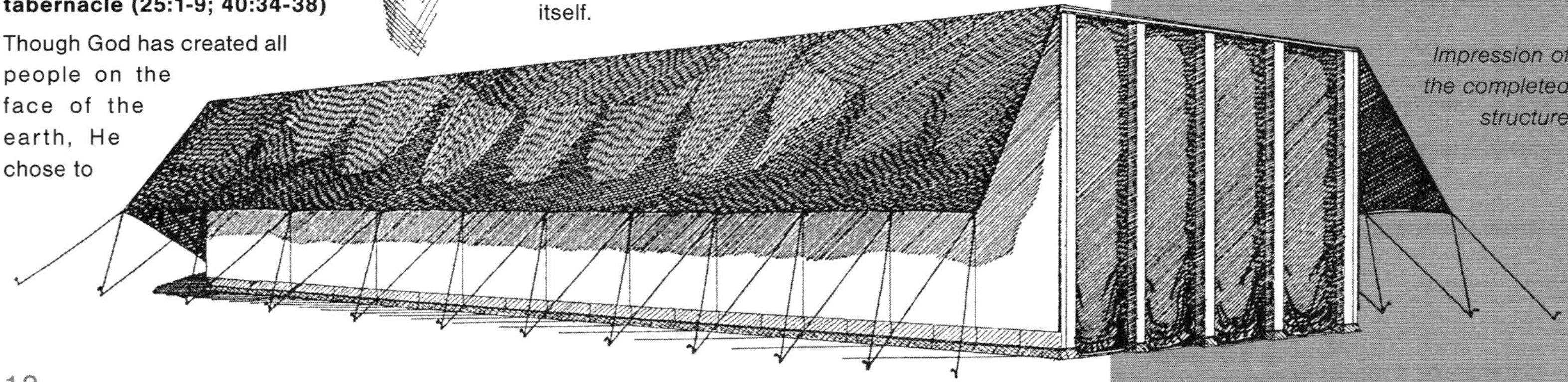

Impression of the completed structure

The outer court (27:9-19; 38:9-20)

The tabernacle structure was positioned inside a courtyard made from hanging curtains. Only the priests were allowed inside the court.

The altar of burnt offering (27:1-8; 38:1-7)

Various sacrifices required under the law were offered on the altar. These provided a "continual burnt offering" before God, showing

Plan of tabernacle and court

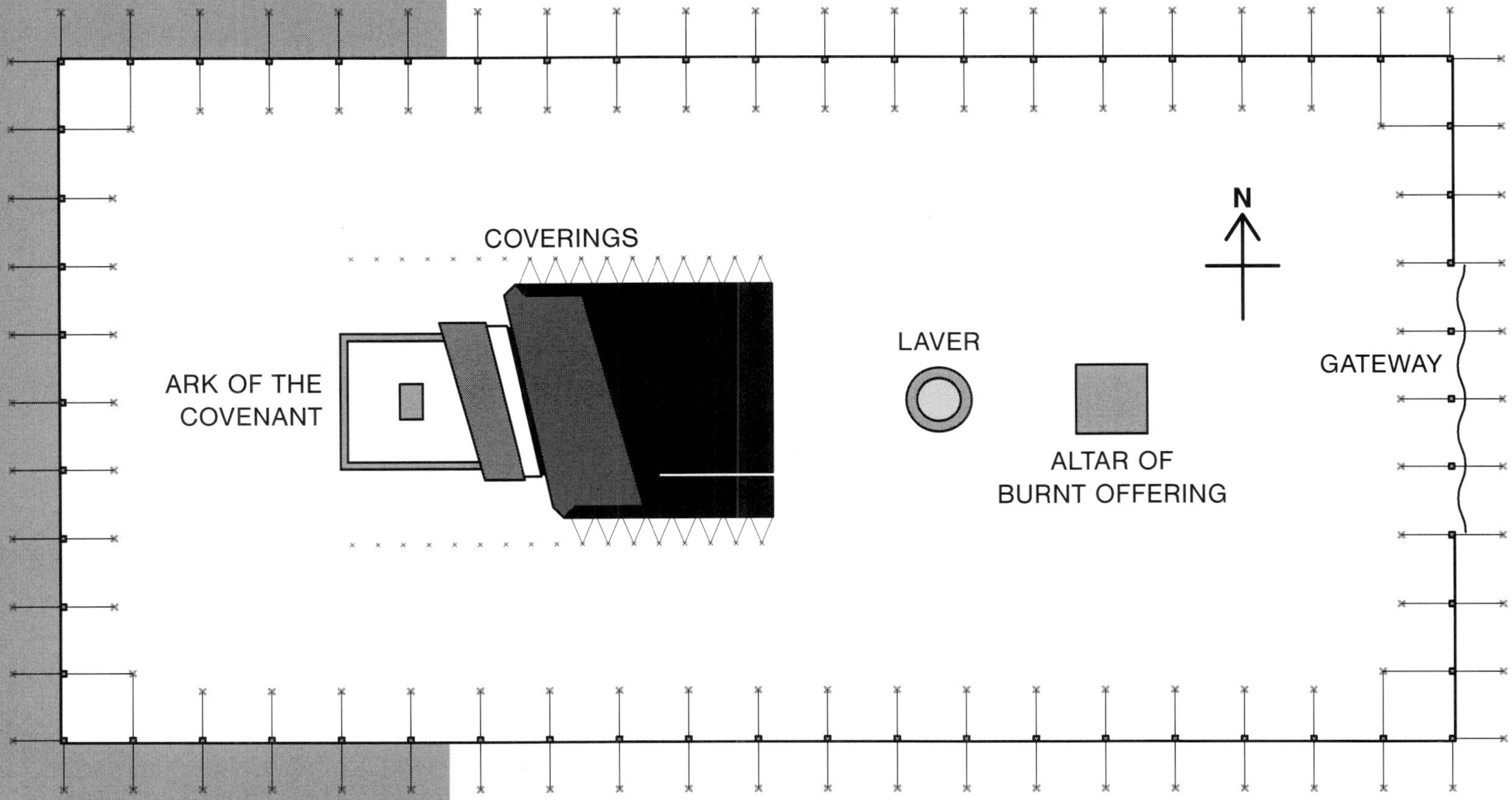

that He must never be forgotten throughout our lives.

The laver (30:17-21; 38:8)

This was a large open container for water, used by the priests to wash before and after every action of service in the tabernacle. It reminds us of the need continually to wash ourselves with the water of God's word if we are to be accepted by Him.

The structure of the tabernacle (26:15-30; 36:20-34)

The tabernacle was so designed that it could be dismantled and re-erected during the wilderness wanderings of the people. In this way God's

Plan of the tabernacle

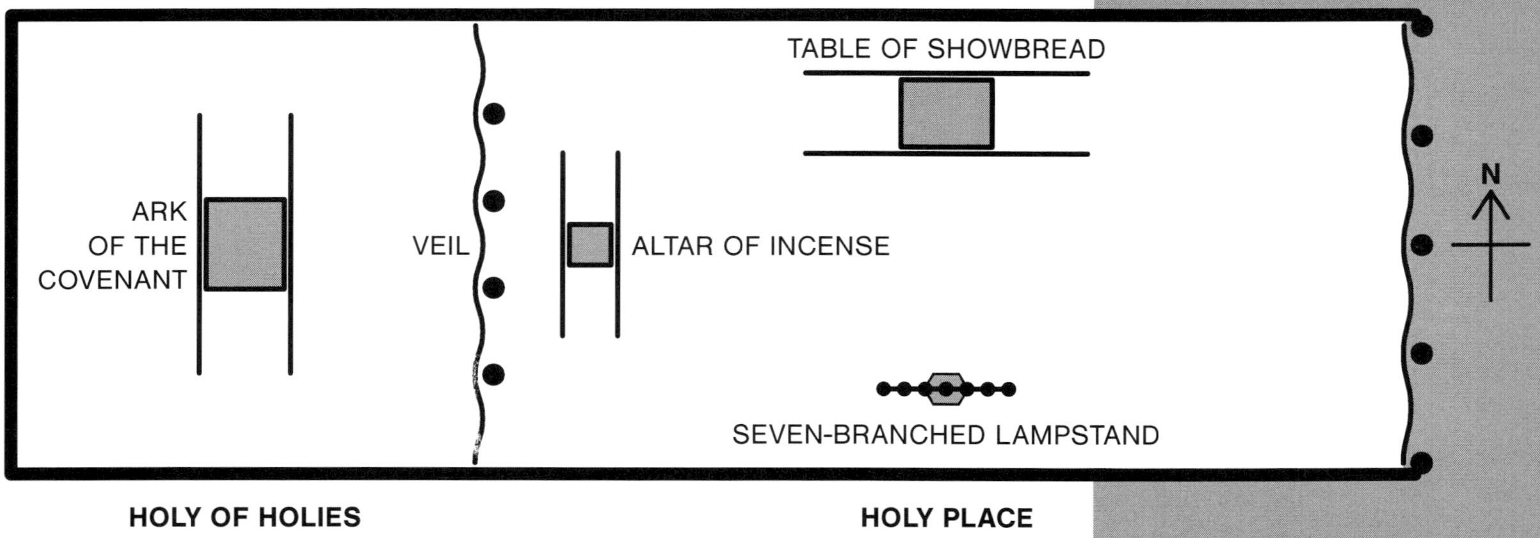

dwelling place was always to be among them, reminding them of His continual presence.

The coverings of the tabernacle (26:1-14; 36:8-19)

Various coverings were used, all having their own part to play in different ways. There were coverings that had important functional uses – to keep out the weather, for example; and there were decorative coverings to beautify the sanctuary. All of them teach significant lessons.

The door (26:36,37; 36:37,38)

Only one entrance was provided to the outer court, and only one doorway was provided into the tabernacle. God has also provided only one way that we can obtain salvation – through the Lord Jesus Christ, who said "I am the door. If anyone enters by me, he will be saved" (John 10:9).

The Holy Place

The first part of the tabernacle building could be entered by even fewer people than the courtyard. Only the priests, whose job it was to look after the lamps and the showbread, and to offer incense, could go in.

The table of showbread (25:23-30; 37:10-16; Leviticus 24:5-8)

Inside the Holy Place was a table bearing twelve loaves, which were renewed weekly. All our food comes from God, and we must offer Him thanks; the Bread of God ultimately was the Lord Jesus Christ, remembered weekly by believers when they break bread in accordance with his command.

The lampstand (25:31-40; 27:20,21; 37:17-24)

The lampstand was also in the Holy Place, providing light continually, day *and* night. Like a stylised tree with branches, it would remind the Israelites of the Tree of Life. Now, God's "word is a lamp to our feet" (Psalm 119:105) and should *always* light the path of our life.

The altar of incense (30:1-10; 37:25-28)

Right against the veil, at the entrance to the Most Holy Place, was the Incense Altar. Here the High Priest burnt incense on behalf of all the people. Beyond the veil was where God's glory dwelt. The only way we can now communicate with God is by prayer, offered up to heaven in Jesus' name.

The veil (26:31,32; 36:35,36)

This separated the Holy Place from the Most Holy Place. It was beautifully embroidered with cherubic figures – a recurring theme in the design of the tabernacle. From the first mention of the cherubim in the Bible we know they are associated with "the way of the tree of life" (Genesis 3:24).

The Most Holy Place

Central to the whole of the layout of the tabernacle, and where the glory of God rested, this room was a perfect cube showing that all the attributes of God Himself are perfect and in harmony with one another.

The Ark of the Covenant (25:10-16; 37:1-5)

Only one item of furniture was placed in the Most Holy Place. Inside the ark were the two tables of stone with the Law engraved on them. Adherence to these principles was the basis of the covenant between God and the nation.

The Mercy Seat (25:17-22; 37:6-9)

Covering the ark was a golden lid supporting two cherubic figures which overshadowed it. Apart from the glory of God which rested between the cherubim and filled the whole room, there was no other source of light.

Setting up the tabernacle (40:1-11,17-33)

As it was necessary to approach the tabernacle in the way God had ordained, so the way it was to be erected was carefully established right from the beginning. It was not for man to decide otherwise, but carefully to follow God's commands.

The tabernacle on the move (Numbers 4)

Each time the tabernacle was dismantled for transportation to the next camping site in the wilderness, detailed instructions had to be meticulously followed. Yet they all taught important lessons about how God wishes to be worshipped.

CHAPTER 03

The purpose of the tabernacle

EXODUS 25:1-9; 40:34-38

JACOB'S *family* went down into Egypt, but it was a *nation* that came out under God's mighty hand in the Exodus. They were still, however, the children of Israel and needed to be welded into a nation. As Moses was their acknowledged leader it would have been easy for them to identify with him and become *his* nation. They needed to be taught that it was God who brought them out, who would watch over them in their journey, and who would bring them into the land He had promised to them and prepared for them.

IN this respect they would be totally unlike any other nation. Other countries had kings and operated as monarchies. Later there would be countries adopting methods of government that involved all the people, known as democracies. Israel was unique and would operate as a *Theocracy*, where the government was based upon God's laws transmitted by His representatives, the priestly tribe of Levi.

To show that God was intimately involved in the nation's welfare, and was guiding it for the ultimate good of its people, He declared in various ways His nearness and abiding presence. This was shown most clearly by the tabernacle.

25:2-7. Though it was designed by God, it was prepared *willingly* by the people of Israel themselves. Because they wanted to know God and be aware of His closeness to them, they had to prepare a place for Him to dwell.

Anyone today who wishes to learn about the God of Israel has to prepare his heart to seek Him, and carefully follow the clear principles He has laid down regarding how He is to be approached by mortal man. The Israelites were not allowed to construct the tabernacle in any way they wished, but had to do it strictly "according to the pattern" received through Moses. God will not be approached now in any way man may choose but only through the "new and living way" prepared through the work of His Son, the Lord Jesus Christ.

God's throne

To approach God is to appreciate heavenly and spiritual things for, as Isaiah declared, "Thus says the LORD: Heaven is my throne, and earth is my footstool" (66:1). So the tabernacle was a representation, not only of God's mercy and grace towards mankind, but of heaven itself – the place where God is praised eternally.

This was explained in the Letter to the Hebrews which gives various details showing how spiritual lessons should be drawn from the information given in the Old Testament about the tabernacle:

> "Christ has not entered the holy places made with hands, which are copies of the true, but into heaven itself, now to appear in the presence of God for us." (9:24)

Thus, to walk from the tribal camps to the tabernacle court, through the Holy Place, and past the veil into the Holiest of all would be like passing from earth to heaven, leaving man's domain and moving into God's. Yet God is holy and "of purer eyes than to behold evil" (Habakkuk 1:13), and man cannot "see [God's] face; for no man shall see me, and live" (Exodus 33:20). So the tabernacle, in the way it was set out, in its materials and in its furnishings, shows how God can be approached. For the Israelites this was accomplished through the medium of the priests, but even they were imperfect examples and displayed the need for someone who could properly represent God to man, and man to God.

Christ is the reality

Only when Jesus came and perfectly obeyed his Father's will did the things shown in pattern in the tabernacle and its service find their reality. They were "a shadow of things to come, but the substance is of Christ" (Colossians 2:17).

8,9. In the book of Exodus there are basically two descriptions of the tabernacle. The first is a specification dictated to Moses by God and passed on by Moses to the people:

> "Then the Lord spoke to Moses, saying: Speak to the children of Israel ... and let them make me a sanctuary, that I may dwell among them." (Exodus 25:1,2,8)

The description of what they were to make starts at the centre of the tabernacle, at its very heart. Fully to understand what the purpose of God's dwelling place among them was to be, it would be necessary to understand first of all the significance of the Ark and the Mercy Seat.

The tabernacle is sometimes called "The tabernacle of the testimony [or witness]" (Exodus 38:21; Acts 7:44). This was partly because the ark contained "the testimony", the stone tablets with the Law written on them, and partly because the tabernacle itself was a testimony (a witness) that the Lord was Israel's God.

The second description is of the construction of the tabernacle. It starts with the making of the curtains which formed the tent, and then proceeds item by item towards the centre, as it would be seen by anyone able to enter the tabernacle once it was completed and erected.

TEST YOURSELF

1. Who was the ruler of the nation of Israel?
2. What attitude of mind was necessary in those who prepared the tabernacle?
3. How can men and women approach God?
4. What was the tabernacle a pattern of?
5. Why is a consideration of the tabernacle important for believers today?

For answers turn to page 66.

CHAPTER 04

The materials and craftsmen

EXODUS 31:1-11; 35:4-35; 36:1-7; 38:21-31

MOSES had been shown "the pattern" of the tabernacle, but it needed the right materials and careful workmen to ensure that it was properly executed and that the final structure would not only be in accordance with God's plans, but would be to the praise of His glory.

31:1-6. God specially selected two men. More than that, He "called [them] by name ... and ... filled [them] with the Spirit of God, in wisdom, in understanding, in knowledge, and in all manner of workmanship" (Exodus 31:2,3). One, skilled in work with textiles was to take care of the curtains and coverings – he was the tentmaker; the other, a skilled carpenter was responsible for the works in metal, wood and stone. This second man was also in overall control of the whole work. They foreshadowed the Lord Jesus, who was known as "the carpenter" (Mark 6:3), and the Apostle Paul, a "tentmaker" (Acts 18:3). This is what we know about these men:

1. They were naturally skilled craftsmen.
2. So that it would have a Godly direction, God increased their skill by filling them with His Spirit. He also put in their heart "the ability to teach" (35:34), allowing them to instruct the other workers about the spiritual significance of their tasks as well as how to fulfil them practically.
3. God called them "by name".

Names are often important in the purpose of God, but on this occasion, when it is specifically recorded that God called them by name, we should expect to see some special significance.

The leading craftsman was "Bezaleel, the son of Uri, the son of Hur, of the tribe of Judah" (31:2). He was from the tribe destined for kingship; his father's name (Uri) means 'enlightenment', which is what happened to Bezaleel when he received Godly wisdom; and his own name means 'God is protection', expressing one of the fundamental principles of the tabernacle.

His assistant, Aholiab, was from the tribe of Dan. His name means 'a father's tent'. This is also what the tabernacle was to be. God was both a Father and a King to the nation of Israel. Aholiab's father was Ahisamach. His name means 'supporting brother' and expresses Aholiab's position in relation to Bezaleel in the work of the tabernacle. He is a good example of one chosen to assist, not to lead. Often this can create tensions which are difficult, but there is no indication in the Bible record that this happened between these two men. Bezaleel was given the overall responsibility and Aholiab was happy to be the 'supporting brother'. This is a lesson which many more could learn with considerable benefit to themselves and to the work they attempt to do.

Wise hearted helpers

The work was not just confined, however, to these two men. Others also assisted them. Because they were prepared to devote their service in this way they are described as being "wise hearted" (31:6; 35:10, KJV). All who offer service to God, because they have come to understand the vanity and emptiness of the world and have chosen instead to honour God, are similarly "wise hearted".

To this group of workmen and under the direction of Moses, the people brought their offerings of the materials to be used in the construction of the tabernacle. Like those who were to do the work, all who brought materials had to do so with "a willing heart" (35:5). As we have already seen on page 6, most of these materials would have originally belonged to Egyptians who gave them to the Israelites to encourage them to leave Egypt quickly. Now they were being devoted to the service of God, teaching every subsequent generation that worldly possessions are provided for us to use to honour God, not to bring glory to men.

The various materials are listed in Exodus 35:5-9.

Gold

Gold is one of the most precious materials in the world. In the tabernacle it was used right in the central part, especially in the Most Holy Place and for the Mercy Seat where the glory of God was to rest. The gold was to be pure. Elsewhere in the Bible gold is used to describe tried and perfected faith. Even then gold is something that "perishes", whereas true faith will be rewarded, and thus will endure (1 Peter 1:7).

Men and women can only approach God in trust and faith in His mercy, never as a result of their own achievements. How appropriate it was, therefore, that this metal should be used for God's dwelling place.

Silver

Silver is not as precious as gold, but still has its place in the provisions of the tabernacle. Silver was used for the shekel, the Israelite coinage. Primarily the shekel was used as a measure for various payments required under the Law. Chief among these was the law of redemption. To instil into the people the fact that everything belongs to God, all newly born animals and children had to be redeemed, or bought back from Him. For children, the redemption cost was measured by "the shekel of the sanctuary", a silver coin.

Silver therefore provided a constant reminder that God had redeemed the people of Israel from Egypt, and had bought them back for His own use.

Bronze

Bronze (or "brass", KJV), is not a precious metal. Nor is it pure, for it is an alloy of different metals (chiefly copper and tin). Elsewhere in the Bible, bronze is associated with the things of man, not of God. Goliath, for example, was clothed in bronze armour (1 Samuel 17:5). He trusted in the armour of men, while David trusted in the Lord, his God.

When Moses was instructed to make a serpent of bronze and place it on a pole, it was to remind those Israelites who had been bitten by snakes that they were dying creatures anyway, because of sin. If they properly appreciated what it meant, they would have seen and understood the necessity for a Saviour, made like themselves, who would fully conquer sin, so that "as Moses lifted up the serpent in the wilderness, even so must the Son of Man be lifted up ... that the world through him might be saved" (John 3:14,17).

The bronze in the tabernacle should therefore have taught the Israelites of their sinfulness, and of their need for redemption.

The importance of these three metals should now be better appreciated. The gold was associated with God, and the bronze with man. Between them was the silver, showing that the only way God and man can meet is on the basis of the redemption made possible through the saving work of the Lord Jesus Christ. In the outer court there was mainly bronze (and some silver). In the Most Holy Place there was only gold. The progression between the two showed how redemption was possible, and teaches us how redemption is possible today by the mercy of God.

Blue

From the various metals we move to the fabrics and textiles used in the tabernacle. In their way they teach the same lesson as the metals and thus reinforce it. Blue is a very fitting representation of heaven, and was used in embroidered work on some of the tabernacle hangings, and a wholly blue material was used to cover some of the sacred furniture when the tabernacle was being transported.

Purple

Purple is a royal colour. It was a difficult colour to produce naturally because the dye came from a small marine animal which was relatively scarce. In the tabernacle it appears between the blue and the red, the two primary colours necessary to mix purple.

Scarlet

Red is the colour of sin, as the prophet shows: "Though your sins are like scarlet, they shall be as white as snow" (Isaiah 1:18).

It is therefore possible to list side by side the metals and textiles used in the tabernacle to show how they both emphasise the same teaching about God's purpose:

Gold	Blue	God, Heaven
Silver	Purple	Christ, Redemption
Brass	Red	Man, Sin

Fine linen

All the materials were the best of their kind. The hangings which were important parts of the tabernacle, were made from "*fine* linen". Later in the Bible it is revealed that "fine linen represents the righteous acts of the saints" (Revelation 19:8). Onto this linen cloth was embroidered a special and intricate design using the three colours, red, blue and purple. This showed that the righteousness is of God's making, and should not be a source of man's pride, but instead of his eternal gratitude.

Goats' hair

Though the coverings of the tabernacle had a symbolic importance, it should not be forgotten that they also had a very practical purpose. The precious materials inside the tabernacle and the fine workmanship of its initial covering needed good and secure weather protection. Three successive coverings were used for this purpose. But they also had a spiritual significance.

The first covering of goats' hair was associated with the special annual occasion when the sins of the whole nation were atoned for during a special ceremony involving the High Priest (see Leviticus 16). It was the only day he was allowed to enter the Most Holy Place, and on that day a goat was used symbolically to carry away the sins of the people. It was "the scapegoat", an idea which has come down to our own day, but has lost most of its real meaning.

This same mercy of God and the ability to repent of sins, knowing they can be forgiven, was shown daily when the teaching of the tabernacle was taken fully to heart.

Rams' skins dyed red

Two rams were used when Aaron and his sons were ordained as priests. The blood from one of them was placed on the tips of their right ears, thumbs and big toes, indicating that as servants of God they should be ready to *hear* His instructions, *do* His will, and *walk* in His ways. The whole tabernacle should teach the same lesson, and therefore the rams' skins would show this, and the fact that they were dyed red would show that man is sinful and needs to devote himself to the ways of God in order to please Him.

Badgers' skins

The translation of this final, outer covering for the tabernacle is very uncertain. Various other animals have been suggested, including porpoises and sea cows. The word basically means a material of a dark red colour, so possibly the exact origin is less important than the fact that it would be an impervious material fulfilling the purpose of keeping the tabernacle dry, and of a colour closely linked with man's sinful state.

The coverings of the tabernacle, therefore, present the same progression from outside to inside as do the metals used throughout its construction. Man is depicted on the outside and, as the means of his redemption is explained by the ram and goat skins, he is led to a consideration of the wonderful purpose of God shown in the intricately embroidered inner curtains.

Acacia wood

Acacia wood is a durable material, well fitted to items needing careful construction. Most probably it was an acacia bush that Moses approached in the desert during his self-imposed exile from Egypt (Exodus 3:1-6). That bush was on fire, but miraculously did not burn away, so that Moses was taught in a special way about the presence of God. He was told to take off his shoes because he was standing on holy ground.

When the tabernacle was later constructed from the same wood, as a dwelling place for God, we would expect Moses to understand its significance as a method of teaching the people the lesson he had already had to learn.

Like Moses in the desert, the priests serving in the tabernacle were barefooted as they moved about the tent where God's presence rested – the Holy Place made it holy ground.

The wood in the tabernacle itself was always covered with gold. God's desire is to dwell with men, but they must be perfected and purified first.

TEST YOURSELF

1. If the bronze and the red coverings both represent sinful man, what did the silver and purple represent?
2. And what did the gold and blue represent?
3. What does the use of silver teach about the work of Jesus?
4. What functional purpose was provided by the tabernacle coverings?
5. Why was only Gold used in the Most Holy Place?

For answers turn to page 66.

CHAPTER 05

The outer court

EXODUS 27:9-19; 38:9-20

THE court which surrounded the tabernacle itself fulfilled a number of functions. It formed a part of the separation between the people and God, and it starts to teach some of the lessons that are gradually developed the nearer an approach is made to the heart of the tabernacle.

IN order to show that God had chosen to dwell among His people, the tabernacle was placed in the centre of their camp. But because man is sinful and God is pure and holy it needed also to be something separate and distinct from the individual tents of the people. Throughout the arrangements for the tabernacle, these two factors are always kept in balance. God was among His people so that He could be approached by them, but they could not approach Him other than in the way He had appointed. The Outer Court was one of the means used to provide this necessary separation and control over access to the presence of God.

A similar idea can be seen in the prayer Jesus taught his disciples. The first phrase, "*Our* Father in heaven", expresses both the intimacy of relationship that can exist between believers and their Creator, and acknowledges that He is in heaven – His ways and thoughts are far beyond those of His creatures. The thought link with prayer is important. In the tabernacle God

WEIGHTS AND MEASURES IN THE TABERNACLE

All the measurements in the tabernacle are based on the cubit. This is one of a range of measurements all based on parts of the human body, and therefore subject to slight differences.

a. Finger or digit (quarter of a handbreadth), 3/4" or 19 mm.

b. Palm or handbreadth (width of hand), 3" or 75 mm.

c. Span (outstretched hand; three handbreadths or half a cubit), 9" or 225 mm.

d. Cubit (elbow to fingertip), 18" or 450 mm.

e. Reed (six cubits), 9' or 2.7 metres.

These are the weights; some of them appear in the tabernacle record:

- Gerah, 0.5 gm.
- Bekah (10 gerahs), 5 gm.
- Shekel (2 bekahs), 10 gm.
- Mina (50 shekels), 500 gm.
- Talent (60 minas), 30 kg.

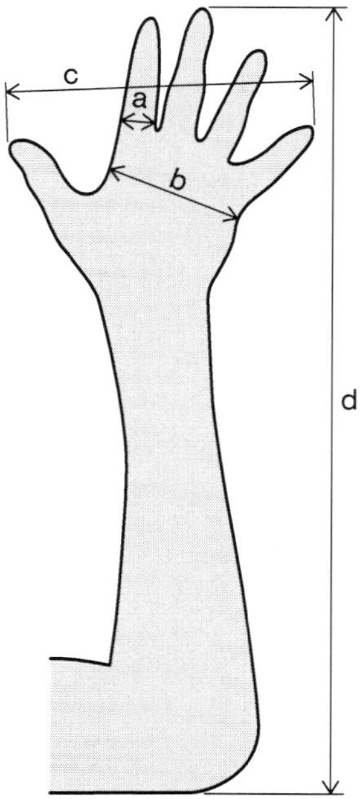

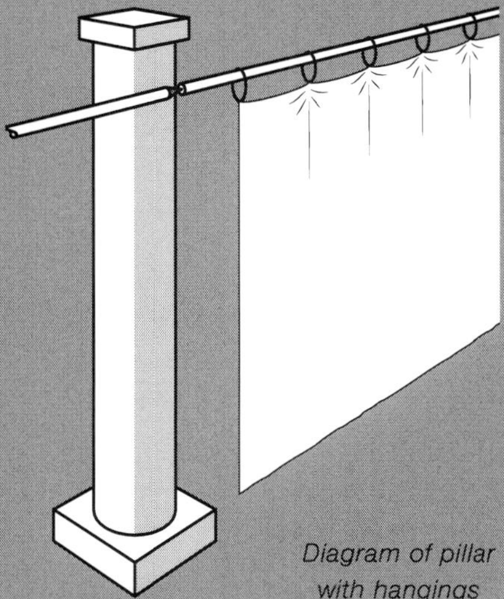

Diagram of pillar with hangings

and man are brought together – on God's terms. Through prayer man is permitted to approach into the presence of God, but never arrogantly or as he decides to do; only in the way God has appointed. To approach before God in prayer through Jesus is like the priests taking the Israelites' offerings, or burning incense on the altar to God.

The necessary reverence and awe which should always exist when God is approached was provided for the Israelites by the special arrangements for the tabernacle site, and by the outer court and its fabric fence. Though these do not exist physically for us today, we are not free to assume God has changed His requirements. He does not accept those who approach without respect or reverence, or by any means other than through the Lord Jesus Christ.

The courtyard itself was sited in the centre of a large area free from the tents of the people. Even the tents of the priests and of Aaron and his own family were kept away from the tabernacle area. The tabernacle was therefore *Holy*, a separated place (for "Holy" means separate), i.e., separate *from* the people and devoted *to* God.

27:9. Even though there were some similarities between the people's tents and the tabernacle, there were also marked differences. Generally theirs would have been dark coloured, but the fence surrounding the outer court was of white "fine linen thread". Anyone walking near it would be silhouetted against its brightness, and this would naturally deter anyone who was inquisitive to see more than the brief glimpse available when taking an animal to be sacrificed.

Verses 10-12. The linen "hangings" were fixed to upright posts supported on the ground at intervals of five cubits (2.5 metres, or 8 feet). There is no mention of the material the "pillars" were made from. Quite probably they were of acacia wood, and stood on bronze bases (or "sockets").

Verses 13-15. The length of the north and south sides of the court was 100 cubits (50 metres); the west side was 50 cubits (25 metres), with the pillars set at 5 cubit (2.5 metre) intervals. The "east side" was also 50 cubits long, but it was divided into three parts:

> "The hangings on one side of the gate [and on the other side, verse 15] shall be fifteen cubits."

Verse 16. This left a central space to be filled by a 20-cubit-wide gateway, also supported on pillars. To distinguish the gateway from the hangings that formed the rest of the boundary to the court, it was made from "blue, and purple, and scarlet yarn, and fine linen thread, made by a weaver".

The design embroidered or woven on the hanging of the gate is not revealed. But because there is a recurring pattern throughout the workmanship in the tabernacle it is possible that the decorative work gave a hint of the later representation of the cherubim. The reasons for this, and the importance of the cherubim, will be considered later.

Verse 17. Wherever we look in the tabernacle, the careful attention to detail can be seen. Every part had its place, and had a special (and often unique) connection to its partner. Like the sockets for the wall panels of the tabernacle building, the sockets for the pillars of the court were probably equipped with a central depression securely to locate the foot of the pillar.

At the head of the pillar, to attach supporting ropes and the hanging curtains, there were "hooks" and "fillets". These were made from silver.

The pillars thus tell a fascinating story. The wood, corruptible like human flesh, was fashioned to be associated with God's dwelling place. As a reminder of man's earthly origin and what this leads him to, the pillar rested on the earth in a socket of brass. Though man needs and seeks companionship, the only true fellowship is the one that stems from an appreciation of God's goodness. The pillars were linked together, not by human ties, but from hooks and bands of "silver".

Verses 18,19. Of the various metals used for the construction of the tabernacle, there was no gold used in the outer court, and no bronze used inside the tabernacle. The only metal common to both areas was silver. Christ by his nature can represent men to God, and by his perfect obedience can represent God to man. Through Christ alone redemption is possible, and we can pray (as the Psalmist did) about the pleasures of serving in the courts of God's house:

> "For a day in thy courts is better than a thousand ... I would rather be a door-keeper in the house of my God than dwell in the tents of wickedness." (Psalm 84:10)

TEST YOURSELF

1. Why was the tabernacle fenced off from the Israelite camp?
2. What does "Holy" mean?
3. What was the predominant metal in the outer court?
4. Why was it appropriate for the outer fence to be linked together by silver fittings?
5. Why was there only one gateway into the courtyard?
6. Who could enter the outer court?

For answers turn to page 67.

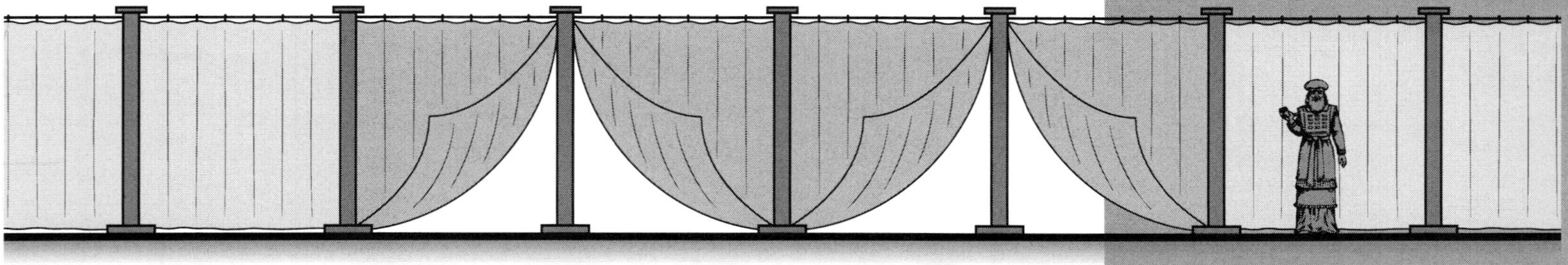

Gateway into outer court

CHAPTER 06

The altar of burnt offering

EXODUS 27:1-8; 38:1-7

IMMEDIATELY inside the gateway, and between the gateway and the tabernacle itself, stood the altar, teaching the important lesson that God cannot be approached except by sacrifice.

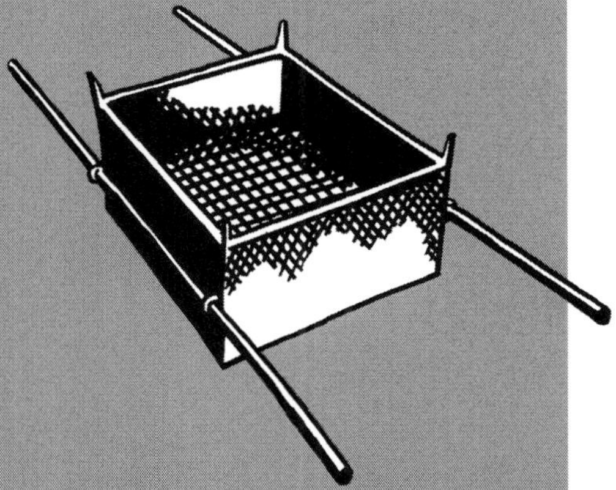

BEFORE the description was given by God to make this altar, He had commanded that they should not be made other than from unhewn stones, nor should they be raised from the ground requiring a flight of steps for the priest to climb to offer sacrifices (Exodus 20:25,26). This was to prevent anyone taking a pride in what they made, and their pride growing into a barrier between themselves and God.

Men like to do things with pomp and dignity, because this boosts their own self-importance. All the provisions in God's arrangements are simple, and do not require any great ceremony. The requirement for baptism, and for baptized believers to remember Jesus' sacrifice in bread and wine are simple but profound examples of God's commands.

The altar for the tabernacle was different because it was built to God's, not to man's, design. Yet the message was the same as the one God wished men to learn when He forbade them making altars other than from unhewn stone.

27:1,2. Within the foursquare camp was a "foursquare" altar. It was five cubits long, five cubits wide, and three cubits high. The height (the top would be about chest high for a man – between 1.25 and 1.5 metres) meant that no steps were necessary. It was made from "acacia wood" and overlaid by "bronze". As we have seen, these fittingly represent humanity, all the things of man: his earthly nature, his corruptibility, and his basic impurity caused by sin.

On the four corners of the altar were "horns". Sacrifices could be tied to these, possibly to keep the carcass above the fire, in much the same way as food is spit-roasted today. For not all the sacrifices had to be completely burnt away; the priests were able to eat some of them.

The altar was placed immediately inside the doorway to the court of the tabernacle. This taught forcefully that everyone approaching the tabernacle was defiled by sin and could approach God only by way of sacrifice or shed blood (see Leviticus 17:11). Though the offerer had to kill his own offering, only the priest could sacrifice it for him. And within the outer court, forming a sacred enclosure entered only by these means, the peace offering was eaten, a sacrificial meal indicating that fellowship had been restored between the offerer and God.

In the same way, we cannot approach God now other than as a result of the perfect sacrifice of Christ. So, when writing to the Hebrews, the apostle said: "We have an altar from which those who serve the tabernacle have no right to eat" (13:10). The provisions of the tabernacle could only lead men to Christ; they could not replace the work he had to do.

Verse 3. "Pans", "shovels", "basons", "forks", and "firepans". These were all the various items of equipment needed by the priests and Levites to deal with the sacrifices. They all had their different uses. Basons were used to catch the blood, forks to remove portions of meat for the priests' use, firepans take some of the fire for use on the incense altar, etc. All these tools were made from "bronze", the predominant material in the outer court.

Verses 4,5. "A grate ... a network of bronze" was made to fit inside the altar as a support to the fire. Its position in "the midst of the altar" suggests that it was somehow fixed half way up, possibly by using the "four bronze rings". This would allow air to circulate beneath the fire, room for the ashes to collect, and space for the fire itself beneath where the sacrifice was tied.

Verses 6,7. One certain use of the rings was for transporting the altar when the Israelites moved camp. It should never be forgotten that the tabernacle was a *portable* sanctuary, teaching of God's presence wherever His people may go. Through the rings were passed wooden "poles", overlaid with bronze like the rest of the altar. These rested on the shoulders of the Levites whose job it was to carry the altar when the camp moved forward.

Verse 8. As a further reminder that the written description is insufficient to build a copy of the tabernacle, God declared, "As it was shown you on the mountain, so shall they make it".

TEST YOURSELF

1. How had God instructed men *not* to make their altars?
2. What was the altar used for?
3. Whose food did it provide?
4. How was the fire supported?
5. What were the staves and rings used for?
6. Is there an altar today for believers in Christ?

For answers turn to page 67.

CHAPTER 07

The laver

EXODUS 30:17-21; 38:8

THE laver was simply a container for water to be used by the priests for cleansing as they went about the tabernacle service, but like everything to do with the tabernacle, a consideration of its function leads to important lessons. In the case of the laver, these are to do with water and washing.

FIRST, however, the material it was made from demands our attention.

30:17,18. The laver was made in two parts, one which contained the water ("the laver"); the other part was made to support it. It was called "the base", or the foot. Both parts were made from "bronze", in keeping with the preponderant use of that material within the outer court of the tabernacle.

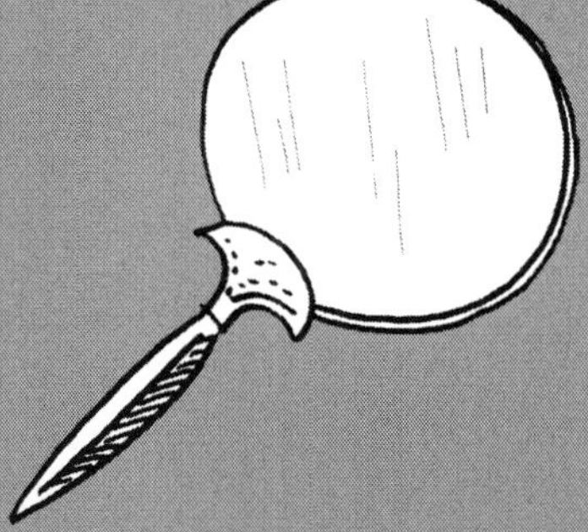

Made from bronze mirrors

It is worth recalling where the bronze came from to construct the laver. In Exodus 38:8 we are told that the women who assembled at the doorway of the temporary tabernacle in great numbers (see KJV margin), brought with them bronze "mirrors". Egypt was a country famed for the beautification of women, and the mirrors would have been obtained while they were in bondage there. In response to the request for materials to build the tabernacle the women brought these very personal articles, forsaking for themselves "that outward adorning of arranging the hair, of wearing gold", for "the hidden person of the heart ... the incorruptible ornament of a gentle and quiet spirit" (1 Peter 3:3,4).

How tragic it was that only a comparatively short time afterwards a similar company of women, who also "assembled at the door of the tabernacle of meeting", had very different motives. Eli's sons, who were desecrating the priesthood in those days, found these women prepared to associate with them in immoral acts in a place where they should have been more aware than ever of the holiness God demands of His people (1 Samuel 2:22).

This giving of their mirrors was symbolic, not only of the women turning from the vain worship of human beauty, but of a desire to serve God actively, and to do His will. The Apostle James wrote about this, possibly with the purpose that we should see what he said against the background of the making of the laver:

> "Be doers of the word, and not hearers only, deceiving yourselves. For if anyone is

a hearer of the word, and not a doer, he is like a man observing his natural face in a mirror: for he observes himself, goes away, and immediately forgets what kind of man he was. But he who looks into the perfect law of liberty and continues in it, and is not a forgetful hearer but a doer of the work, this one will be blessed in what he does."

(James 1:22-25)

Looking into God's word is very different from looking into a mirror. A mirror reflects the face looking into it. In God's word we see, not our own, but God's characteristics.

Returning to the laver, Moses was told to "put it between the tabernacle of meeting and the altar". This was not because that was the most convenient place for a vessel of that kind. Nothing was placed casually among the different parts of the tabernacle. Remembering that to walk from the Israelites' tents to the Holy of Holies was to walk from man's domain to God's, from death to life, the position of the laver teaches an important lesson. It was placed in a position where it could only be approached *after* passing the altar and *before* entering the tabernacle.

There is no description of the size or shape of the laver, so the visual evidence of "the pattern" Moses saw in the Mount would be crucial for Bezaleel and his workers to make this particular item. Nor is there any description of how the water was brought to fill it. Once the nation was in the land, provision was made for "woodcutters and water carriers" (Joshua 9:21), but while the nation was in the wilderness no information is given about the arrangements to fill or replenish the laver.

Baptism and forgiveness

Verse 19. The water contained in the laver was to be used only by the priests – "Aaron and his sons". They had to wash "their hands and their feet". Ceremonial washing of this kind has an important purpose. Man's ways and his doings are astray from God's, and he needs cleansing. "Wash me thoroughly", said the Psalmist, "cleanse me from my sin" (51:2). Any approach to God must involve an understanding of this natural state of man, and the recognition that only God, after honest repentance, can forgive sins.

Verses 20,21. Under Christ individuals also need washing. Baptism, symbolically cleansing a believer from his former sins, would be valueless unless Christ had first been sacrificed. We are buried (in water) into his death and resurrection, becoming part of one Family of God, growing into His house. The apostles were sent out by Jesus to "preach the gospel to every creature. He that believes *and is baptized* shall be saved" (Mark 16:16).

Baptism is an early stage in the service of God. Just like the priests had to wash in the laver *before* they could minister in any part of the tabernacle service – "when they go into the tabernacle ... or when they come near the altar to minister" – so the disciple has to be baptized *before* he can commence full service for God.

The importance of this command is stressed when the punishment for not upholding it is examined. The priests had to do it "lest they die". Nor was it a command applying only to Aaron and his generation; it was "a statute for ever to them ... throughout their generations". How they would die is not revealed. Possibly the anger of God would break out against them, as it did against Korah, Dathan and Abiram when they disregarded the provisions of tabernacle worship; or it may be a description of their eternal destiny if they disobeyed.

In this way, however, the importance of baptism today as well as in the days of the apostles is forcefully declared. Jesus' command to his disciples went on to say "he who does not believe will be condemned".

Sanctification

But water is also used in the Bible to teach other lessons. Just as baptism is not the end, but the beginning of a life of service to God, the continual washing by the priests at the laver holds a message about our necessary *daily* commitment to the things of God. Jesus gave himself for those who would follow him, "that he might sanctify and cleanse [them] with the washing of water by the word" (Ephesians 5:26). How can we possibly serve God acceptably if we do not regularly remind ourselves of what He has spoken about His requirements, and about His purpose?

Finally, on the subject of the laver, it is necessary to comment upon something we are not told about. All the other items of furniture associated with the tabernacle had provision for being covered during transportation, but not the laver. Perhaps this could be a way of God revealing to us that this important step by means of which a right relationship can be entered into, is always available, and furthermore is a constant witness to the salvation God promises to all who are prepared to turn to Him to cleanse their ways.

TEST YOURSELF

1. What was the laver used for?
2. Who used it?
3. What parts of their body did the priests wash?
4. Where did the bronze come from in the first place?
5. How can God's word be likened to a mirror?
6. Do you spend more time looking in a mirror than considering the things to do with God and His purpose?

For answers turn to page 68.

CHAPTER 08

The structure of the tabernacle

EXODUS 26:15-30; 36:20-34

THE way the tabernacle 'building' was constructed has fascinated anyone with a practical turn of mind, though there are sufficient important gaps in what has been revealed to prevent anyone being absolutely certain that he has got it right. Moses' vision in the Mount was the key to the Israelites being able to construct it. In the absence of that information we have to be careful not to be dogmatic about things where there is only partial information in the scriptures.

AS we have seen earlier, what has been revealed is sufficient for us to appreciate the *purpose* behind the various provisions and details of the tabernacle.

"Fitly framed together"

Because the children of Israel were leading a nomadic life, wandering at God's direction through the Sinai desert, the tabernacle was not a permanent structure. The description we have focuses on the way each of the various parts was distinct, yet how it was possible for them to be brought together to form a unified whole. Each part had its own unique method of attachment to its neighbour. Drawing upon this information and applying it to the way individual believers are linked together within the body of Christ, the apostle Paul wrote about the "household of God ... being joined together ... a habitation of God in the Spirit" (Ephesians 2:19-22).

Just as the believers have God and His Son at the centre of their lives, so in the tabernacle everything focused upon the dwelling presence of God in the Most Holy Place. God was both the architect of the tabernacle, and the reason for its existence. Ultimately, like the body of believers in Christ, it was held together by His commands, made into tenons and sockets, rings and bars. The apostle also wrote about this, speaking first of Christ: who is "the Head, from whom all the body, nourished and knit together by joints and ligaments, grows with the increase which is from God" (Colossians 2:19).

As God is the Author of all things, it is not surprising that what He commanded for the tabernacle has its counterpart in the natural and the spiritual creation. Paul was able to take the principles behind the connections in the tabernacle and speak of them as patterns

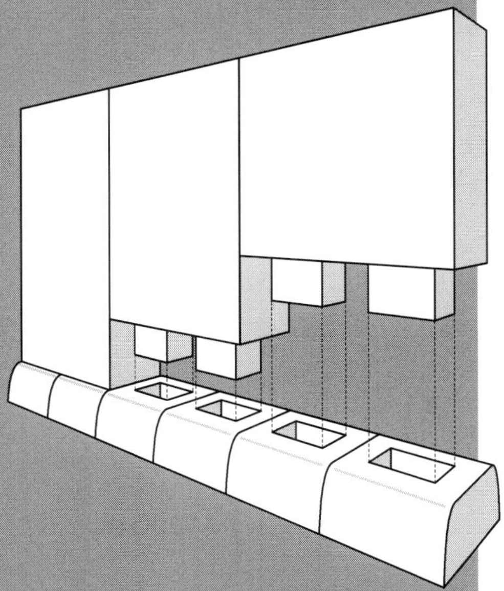

of the way believers are linked together in fellowship, and also to show how the body of Christ is patterned upon a human body, where muscles, joints and vessels connect the various parts, supplying all the different needs, yet with a common purpose.

When examining the tabernacle these important truths should not be forgotten.

26:15,16. The main walls of the tabernacle were formed from "boards" made from "acacia wood". Straight away we run into a problem. These boards were ten cubits long, one and a half wide, and (probably) a span thick (5 metres × 750 mm × 225 mm). To make them out of solid wood would need very large trees, and the finished board would be extremely heavy. As the boards were all covered with gold, this would further add to their weight (see verse 29). As this seems to militate against the ready portability of the tabernacle, other ideas have been suggested. The RSV translates this section like this: "You shall make upright *frames* ... of acacia wood." The idea here is that a sort of ladder with the same overall dimensions would be much lighter, and could be constructed from smaller timbers.

However we may feel about the problem, scripture does not provide us with sufficient information to be certain, and it is therefore wrong to be dogmatic. The spiritual lessons are more important for us today than exactly how everything was able to fulfil its practical purpose.

Fellowship explained

Verses 17-21. At the bottom of each board were "two tenons". These located into silver "sockets" laid directly onto the desert floor. The idea of fellowship really commences here. The Hebrew word for tenon literally means 'hand'. The boards of the tabernacle were like individual believers standing upright in the presence of God, holding out both hands ready to be grasped. Holding these 'hands' tightly were the silver sockets helping to unite the whole structure. We have already seen how silver represents redemption, and it is only right that believers are joined together by the common redemption they have in Christ.

There is no distinction between the boards used round the Holy Place from those used round the Most Holy Place. They were interchangeable, being constructed to the same specification. So there should be no distinction between individual believers in Christ, for they are all "members of one another" (Romans 12:5).

Verses 22-25. The only difference between the boards occurs at the corners. Many people have puzzled over exactly what is meant by "two boards ... coupled together at the bottom, and ... at the top by one ring". The RSV says: "they shall be *separate* beneath, but *joined* at the top"! In some way not fully revealed, there was a special arrangement at the corner which also continued to express the idea of fellowship, for the boards were "coupled" together (the same word is translated "fellowship" in Psalm 94:20).

Verses 26-29. Apart from the special boards at the rear corners of the tabernacle, the boards were fixed at the foot by means of the tenons and sockets, but not connected at the top. To counteract this inherent instability, five wooden "bars" covered with gold passed through golden rings on the outside of the boards. Exactly how these were arranged is not revealed. It is unlikely that each bar would be 30 cubits (15 metres) long, so possibly they were only half the length of the tabernacle.

Of one of the bars, "the middle bar ... in the midst of the boards", we are told that it reached "from end to end". We do not know whether this means that somehow it was passed through the thickness of each board as a final feature, locking all the boards tightly together, or whether, as the central of the five bars, it was half way up the height of the tabernacle. However it worked, its effect was to unify the structure and make it secure.

Verse 30. The erection of the tabernacle – the actual method of fitting all the parts together, like following an assembly diagram, had to be done "according to its pattern which you were shown on the mountain".

TEST YOURSELF

1. Why is it not possible to construct the tabernacle today from the information given in the Bible?
2. The methods used to join together the various parts teach important lessons. What principle do they explain?
3. What other figure (in addition to believers being like a tabernacle or temple) is used in the New Testament to describe fellowship?
4. How do the various structural parts of the tabernacle relate to believers in Christ?
5. Do you see the need for individual believers to associate together in fellowship?

For answers turn to page 68.

CHAPTER 09

The coverings of the tabernacle

EXODUS 26:1-14; 36:8-19

THE tabernacle coverings each performed an important function. From the inner, highly decorated, linen curtains, which displayed figures of cherubim, to the outer covering of badgers' skins, the need for weather protection and for spiritual education was fulfilled.

THOUGH it would be true to say that there were a succession of coverings described in scripture, all with a specific purpose, the first covering stands out by reason of its intimate connection with the tabernacle framework.

Though the completed structure enclosed by the outer court was known as the "tabernacle [Hebrew, *ohel*, meaning 'tent'] of meeting", the gold-plated timber framework and the first covering formed "The tabernacle" (Hebrew, *mishkan*, meaning 'dwelling place').

Strangely, it was a provision for the whole congregation, although strictly speaking it was *God's* dwelling place, His sanctuary.

Left: The inner curtain hung 1 cubit clear of the ground

Right: The two groups of curtains were joined over the veil

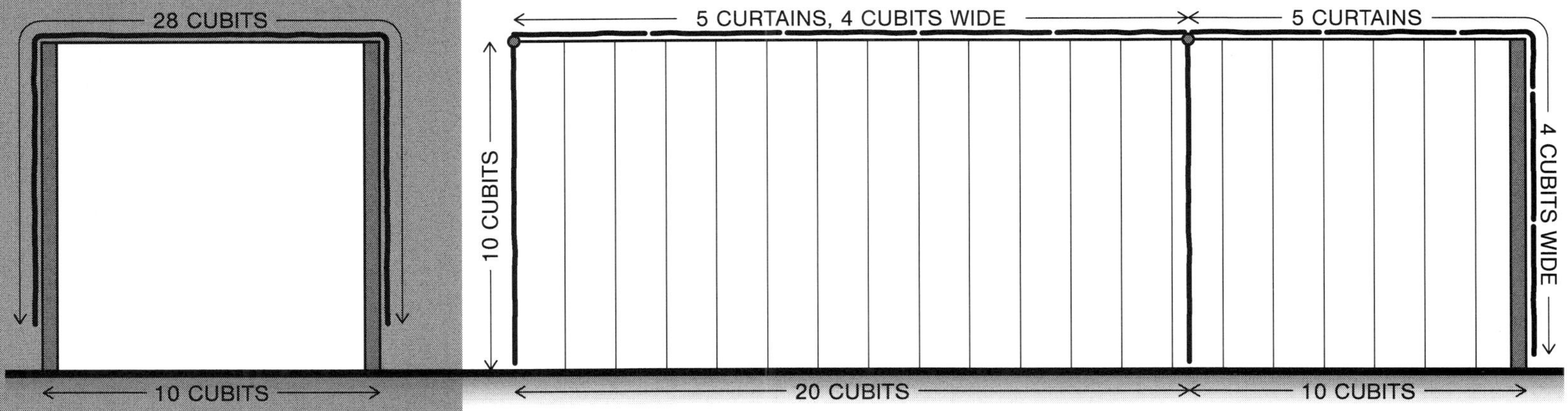

The first covering

26:1. "You shall make the tabernacle". The importance of the first covering is here emphasised. The dwelling place for God would be incomplete without it. Of all the textiles used in the tabernacle, this covering and the veil stand out because they were of "artistic designs" (cunning work, KJV). The material was "fine linen thread" woven or embroidered with designs based on the cherubim in colours of blue, purple and scarlet. If the boards of the walls were solid, the only place the intricate design could be seen from inside the tabernacle would be on the ceiling. If, instead, the structure was more of an open-work frame the design on the linen covering would become an integral part of the internal decoration.

Verses 2,3. Ten separate curtains were made to the same specification, each 28 cubits (14 metres) long and 4 cubits (2 metres) wide. What a task it would have been to weave or embroider curtains of this size! It would clearly have been impractical to attempt to work on anything any larger. The ten curtains were then divided into two groups, five curtains being sewn together. This would have made two curtains each 28 cubits (14 metres) long and 20 cubits (10 metres) wide. These very heavy articles needed to be transported and lifted up onto the framework of the tabernacle, a job needing a group of strong men to accomplish it.

Verses 4-6. A firm connection was needed between the two sets of curtains. This was provided by attaching to the edge of each set 50 blue loops, through which golden clasps were passed, described as "fifty clasps of gold". As the diagrams show, the dimensions of the curtains and of the tabernacle were such that the curtains hung clear of any damage from contact with the ground, and were joined together over the veil which separated the Holy Place from the Most Holy Place.

Curtains of goats' hair

Verses 7-11. The "covering" (*ohel*) over the "tabernacle" (*mishkan*) was provided by eleven goats' hair curtains in two groups, one of five curtains joined together, the other of six. Like the linen curtains, these were linked by loops and clasps, but here the similarity ends. The material or colour of the loops is not described, but the clasps were not gold, only bronze. We have already seen that no bronze was

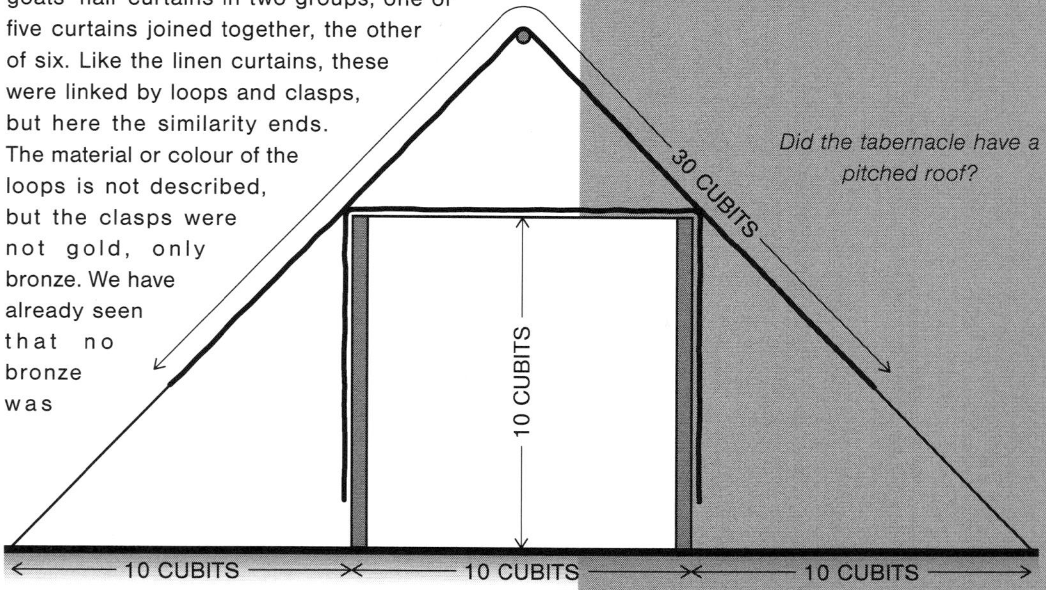

Did the tabernacle have a pitched roof?

HOW WAS THE TABERNACLE ROOF SUPPORTED?

Anyone who has done any camping will appreciate that four sets of heavy curtains draped over a distance of 10 cubits (5 metres) need some form of support. The problem is that no supports are mentioned in the specification. Disposal of rainwater would also be difficult from a roof that would sag in the middle. The middle bar described in connection with the tabernacle boards has been seen as a possible solution. Because it is described as "in the midst of the boards" and reaching "from end to end" (26:28), some people have thought it was a ridge pole. This only serves to create a further problem, because there is nothing specified in the description of the tabernacle to hold it up!

Supporters of the flat-roof theory say that as there is no description of poles and supports, the roof must have been flat; while supporters of the pitched-roof theory say that a flat roof would be unworkable unless there were also some supports to stop the coverings from sagging and pulling in the tops of the walls.

Clearly, if we were meant to know which theory is correct, the information would exist to tell us. More than anything else this indicates that the descriptions, even though they are repeated (for emphasis?, like Pharaoh's dreams, see Genesis 41:32), are not given so that it is possible to build a replica of the tabernacle, but so that we can learn the important lessons it teaches about how men and women can approach God correctly.

associated with the Holy Place or Most Holy Place, so the same progression noted from the courtyard into the presence of God also applies to the coverings of the tabernacle. The innermost layer was most closely related to God, while the outer layers had reference to the state of mortal human beings.

The other difference between the first two sets of curtains is that the goats' hair curtains had an extra curtain to be doubled "at the forefront of the tent". Possibly this was to provide a means for covering the opening of the tabernacle in times of bad weather. It would certainly help to hide the decorated curtains completely from view. As the goats' hair curtains were longer than the linen curtains (30 cubits compared with 28) the linen curtains would be hidden at the sides and rear also.

Verses 12,13. These two verses are extremely difficult. Why there should be half a curtain left at the rear to hang over the tabernacle, and only a cubit at each end of the curtains to hang over the sides is a mystery. Some commentators have attempted to answer the difficulty by also solving another problem. They have queried how the roof of the tabernacle was supported, as no information about this appears in the text. See box alongside for more details about this difficulty.

Even if the tabernacle had a pitched roof, the problem of the goats' hair curtains remains. If the coverings (*ohel*) were separated from the tabernacle (*mishkan*), the diagram opposite shows a way that the verses can be harmonised, but this would leave the embroidered curtains visible from the outside by anyone entering the outer court, and somewhat less protected.

Verse 14. On top of the goats' hair curtains were two further coverings. No sizes are given for these, nor does it appear that they were made in two sections and then joined together. For weather protection they would need to cover the open-work joint between the first two sets of curtains, so they were probably well joined together into one large (and very heavy!) curtain.

The first of these two curtains was made from rams' skins dyed red. The word translated "red" is the Hebrew word *Adam*, showing that man was being reminded of his sinfulness and his own need for "a covering" for his sin to be provided graciously by God. The covering provided for Adam was "coats of skin" (Genesis 3:21). For believers, the perfect covering is Jesus Christ.

TEST YOURSELF

1. How were the various sets of curtains divided?
2. What is significant about this division?
3. The first covering was similar to what other part of the tabernacle?
4. How were the coverings supported?
5. How were the two innermost coverings joined together?

For answers turn to page 69.

CHAPTER 10

The door

EXODUS 26:36,37; 36:37,38

THE tabernacle was not to be open to view from within the outer courtyard, for a special hanging curtain was provided to screen the interior and to allow access only for those authorised to enter.

26:36. The curtain was presumably 10 cubits wide by 10 cubits high (about 5 metres × 5 metres). That was the size of the opening, and the curtain was made to screen it. Like the innermost covering to the tabernacle, it was of "fine linen thread made by a weaver", in blue, purple and scarlet. As there is no indication of the design worked upon it, it could possibly have been similar to the hangings at the gate of the outer court, where the same description is given.

Verse 37. The curtain was supported by "five pillars of acacia wood". The pillars were covered with gold, yet stood on bronze bases, like those used for the supports to the boundary of the outer court. The two preponderant metals thus met at the doorway to the tabernacle. In the courtyard there was mainly bronze, and in the tabernacle mainly gold. There is thus a hint here that mortal man (bronze) can have righteousness (gold) ascribed to him.

There was only one way into the tabernacle. Entry was thus carefully controlled. Nor could just anyone go in. Entry was carefully restricted. Careful preparations in accordance with God's commands were necessary, and even those few who were allowed to enter, could be debarred from entering if anything occurred to make them unclean.

These were the aspects Jesus referred to about God's sheepfold. He said:

> "I am the door. If anyone enters by me, he will be saved, and will go in and out and find pasture." (John 10:9)

As no-one will be able to claim undisputed entry, because no-one can perfectly fulfil God's conditions, He has extended His grace towards men and women. Grace is undeserved favour, a blessing bestowed on someone who does not merit it. Throughout scripture grace is represented by the number five, and in the case of the doorway into the tabernacle, by the five gold-covered pillars that supported the curtain.

TEST YOURSELF

1. What other linen hanging was like the door to the tabernacle?
2. Could every Israelite man and woman enter the tabernacle through the door?
3. How is access to the presence of God controlled today for those who wish to approach Him?

For answers turn to page 69.

CHAPTER 11

The Holy Place

TEST YOURSELF

1. What provides the bridge between man and God? between earth and heaven?
2. In the developing history of God's dealings with His people, which period is represented by the Holy Place?
3. What lesson did the regular work of the Holy Place teach the Israelites, and what does it teach us today?

For answers turn to page 70.

THE Holy Place was entered daily by the officiating priest, whose job it was to tend to the lamp, make the weekly changes to the table of showbread, or offer incense on the incense altar.

PROPERLY to appreciate the Holy Place, therefore, it is necessary to see it as representing the work of the Lord Jesus Christ and generally also the period when the Law of Moses operated. Sacrifices had to be offered daily in those times, when God wanted men to appreciate that there needed to be "one sacrifice for sins *for ever*". The fact that the lamps needed daily attention and that the showbread needed replacing weekly, should have assisted them in understanding these things.

Similarly, even though by the supreme sacrifice of Christ we can be freed from the need for regular sacrifices, we are constantly reminded of man's inability to find salvation by any other means; and of the corruption of sin, daily, weekly, and throughout our lives.

In the Letter to the Hebrews further information is given about the tabernacle and the important lessons to be gained from it by believers today. The various parts of the tabernacle are used in the Bible to teach these different things:

The outer court	The Holy Place	The Holy of Holies
Mortals needing forgiveness	Mortals forgiven	Immortals
All mankind	The Lord Jesus Christ	God
The World	The Ecclesia	Heaven
Times before the Law	Times under the Law	Times under Christ

CHAPTER 12

The table of showbread

EXODUS 25:23-30; 37:10-16

OF the three items of furniture in the Holy Place, the table of showbread seems to have the least useful purpose. Twelve loaves of bread were placed on it every sabbath day (i.e., the seventh day of the week – Saturday). When they were replaced, the old ones had to be eaten by the priests ("Aaron and his sons") in the Holy Place (see Leviticus 24:9). Old bread is not normally tasty or a privilege to eat, so the significance of the act must have been of more importance than the nourishment it provided.

BY eating it, they were sharing in an offering that had been made to God. They were sharing food dedicated to God; it was holy, and they needed to be holy too.

25:23,24. The table was not very large: two cubits long, by a cubit wide, and standing one and a half cubits high (1 metre × 50 cm × 75 cm). Made from acacia wood, it was covered with gold and had as an ornamental feature, "a moulding of gold all around". This same feature occurs on the altar of incense (see chapter 37:26) and on the ark of the covenant (see chapter 25:11). Like other aspects repeated in the different parts of the tabernacle, the provision of the Ark is anticipated in part by the lessons of the table of showbread.

The showbread needed replacing weekly, whereas in the ark was placed a golden pot of manna (Hebrews 9:4) which, being in the presence of God, never corrupted, and certainly never needed replacing.

Verses 25-28. The feature of the golden moulding was also repeated on the table of showbread itself. Around the table there was a border, and this border also had its own "moulding". Though the table legs are not described (they are just called "feet"), where they were fastened to the top were placed four rings, through which carrying poles could be passed. These poles, like the rest of the table, were made from acacia wood, covered with gold.

Verse 29. Various implements are listed, and were also made from gold – "dishes ... pans ... pitchers ... and bowls". The exact function of all these items is not revealed, but they were associated closely with the table of showbread. Perhaps they were the implements used for baking the bread in the first place.

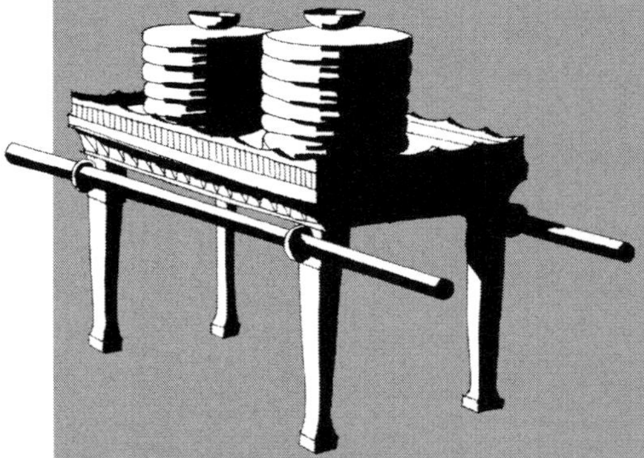

Verse 30. Finally, the purpose of the showbread is described: "You shall set the showbread on the table before me always". The bread was to be constantly in the presence of God, and it was to be *show*-bread. What did it show? It was, of course, always *on show* before God, but it also showed God's desire for fellowship with men. Fellowship is most intimately declared when the fellowship, or communion (meaning sharing or participation) meal is eaten. This was done weekly by the priests when, on behalf of the nation, they ate of the loaves that had been "on show" for the preceding week.

From the record in Leviticus we can learn the procedure for making, setting out and changing the loaves. The loaves were of "fine flour" and were unleavened (24:5). The nature of the fellowship they represented is shown by the careful description of how they and the table were made. They were to be set out "on the *pure* table before the Lord" (verse 6).

The loaves, twelve in number, were placed in two piles, six in each pile; and the piles were topped by a small bowl containing "pure frankincense". It was placed there "for a memorial" (verse 7). As bread throughout scripture is an emblem of human labour (see Genesis 3:19), these loaves were representative of the desire of God's nation (made up of twelve tribes, equalling the number of loaves) to serve Him. This service, in remembrance of His continuing goodness, is pleasing to God. As frankincense was used with some of the offerings and in the holy incense itself, it was an ingredient declaring the satisfaction God receives from wholehearted service.

Bread of life

Ultimately, Jesus declared that he is "the bread *of life*" (John 6:48). His service, because it was totally acceptable before God, does not need to be repeated again and again: it never grew stale, nor did it need replacing with a renewed commitment.

By contrast, even though we are freed from the necessity always to offer sacrifices to atone for our sins, we do need constantly to remember what has been achieved on our behalf. So there is a "memorial" provided for believers in Christ. They share bread and wine together – tokens of Jesus' death and resurrection, and tokens of the promise that humankind, and the earth itself, will be freed from the restraints imposed as a result of sin, and become a praise to God who created them. This "memorial" meal, like the priests' meal of showbread, is usually eaten once a week, on the *first* day of the week, commemorating Jesus' resurrection; not like them on the last day of the week, showing they were involved with something that was passing.

TEST YOURSELF

1. What does bread represent in the Bible?
2. Why were there twelve loaves?
3. Whose food were they?
4. Who ate the loaves?
5. What did this meal represent?
6. Why was it called "showbread"?

For answers turn to page 70.

CHAPTER 13

The lampstand

EXODUS 25:31-40; 27:20,21; 37:17-24

ON the opposite side of the Holy Place from the table of showbread stood the lampstand. Because of the heavy coverings over the tabernacle, even in the desert heat and the strong sunlight, it would be very dark inside the tent. The absence of natural light required that there should be a light so that the priests could see to carry out their daily work. But the real reason is more important than this.

BECAUSE the Holy Place was designed to show the Israelites the dedication God wished them to have in their service to Him, the fact that light was only available from the lampstand teaches that, with respect to our lives in God's sight, we must walk only in His light.

The Psalmist wrote, "Your word is a lamp to my feet, and a light unto my path" (119:105). Other circumstances can lead us to a consideration of the things of God, but only in His word can we learn about Him and His purpose with the world, centred in the Lord Jesus Christ. As Jesus was the "bread of life", so he is also "the light of the world" (John 8:12).

25:31. The lampstand was a unique piece of craftsmanship. Made from "pure gold", it was not moulded or cast, but made of "hammered work". Could this be an indication of how God's word can work upon the characters of those who read it? There is never a sudden transformation from a state of living according to the pleasures of the world to living according to the commandments of God. Like something being carefully shaped by gradual beating against a former, human characters can be altered to become more like that of the Lord Jesus, if they are shaped in conformity with him.

The lampstand was a stylised tree. It had a trunk ("shaft"), "branches", buds (or "knobs"), and "flowers". The type of tree it was based on is not revealed, but the similarity with Aaron's rod, which budded, blossomed and fruited (Numbers 17:8), could suggest that this also was like an almond tree.

The tree of life?

But there are also other clues that could link the lampstand, not only with Aaron's rod, but with the tree of life mentioned at the beginning and end of the Bible account (Genesis 2:9; Revelation 22:2). When Adam and Eve were

banished from the garden of Eden, cherubim were placed "to guard [i.e., to preserve] the way of the tree of life" (Genesis 3:24). The provisions made at that time for the restoration of man to loving fellowship with God are found presented in physical form in the tabernacle, so that Israel could be taught how the breach with God could be healed.

The clues consist of the cherubim and the glory of God which dwelt in the Most Holy Place. God's glory is like "a flaming sword" (Genesis 3:24), because although it can enlighten men, it can also destroy them when they rebel against His will.

Verses 32-36. From the main shaft of the lampstand were formed six "branches". These were also decorated with "knobs and flowers", continuing the tree theme. Together with the central shaft these terminated in *seven* bowls. From the days in the creation week, seven (the day God rested – Genesis 2:2) is normally associated with completion or perfection. And so it is here, for God would not allow in His dwelling place among men something that was not able to portray the complete ability of His word to enlighten the hearts and minds of men, and to reveal to them His purpose.

"The light of the world"

Apart from the weight of gold used in its manufacture, no dimensions are given for the lampstand. We do not know how high it stood, how wide the branches spread, or how large the lamps were. Yet everything about it was complete: there were seven branches, and it was made from one *whole* talent, of *pure* gold. Known to the Jews as the *Menorah*, it is almost as common as the Star of David or the spies carrying the huge bunch of grapes as a symbol representing Israel.

How tragic it is that God's nation fails to recognise Jesus who likened himself to the lampstand, lighting not only the Holy Place, but the world as well, if men will allow him.

Verses 37,38. On each of the bowls at the end of the branches was placed an oil lamp. As everything else associated with the lampstand was made from gold, we should expect that these were also, though the information is not contained in the record. It would be easier to keep the lamps burning continually with seven of them, for when they were being replenished with oil and the wicks trimmed, they could be attended to one at a time, leaving the remainder alight. This job was the work of the priests – "Aaron and his sons" (Exodus 27:21).

To carry out this work, "wick-trimmers and their trays" were also made from gold, and kept beside the lampstand. On the table of showbread were loaves made from "*fine* flour". In the lamps on the lampstand was "*pure* oil of pressed olives" (27:20). For anything to be pure and refined, fit for service before God, it needs to have all the impurities removed. The lampstand itself had to be fashioned "according to the pattern" (25:40), and gradually the shape and the intricate decoration would have come to life under the skilled hands of Bezaleel and his assistants. So also with the ingredients of the consumable items for the tabernacle service. The flour was finely ground, and the oil for the lamps was produced from finely pressed olives. For God only the best, diligently carried out, is good enough.

Verses 39,40. The whole lampstand: the base, the shaft and the branches, together with all the decoration on them, was made *in one piece*, from "a talent of pure gold" (verse 39). Anyone with any knowledge of fine goldsmith's work knows that the skill does not exist today to produce such an article. The weight of gold involved, together with the craftsmanship needed to produce it, would have made the lampstand a priceless article, able to command preposterous sums of money on the world market.

Though it is fitting that something so unique should also be valued highly by the world, it is ironical that what it represented is so often treated as a thing of no value at all. Men see God's word as a collection of quaint stories. But in reality it also is something beyond price and of inestimable value.

TEST YOURSELF

1. Of what other incidents in the Bible does the lampstand remind you?
2. Who tended the lamps?
3. What fuel was burned in the lamps?
4. What light is available today for those who wish to learn about God?

For answers turn to page 71.

CHAPTER 14

The altar of incense

EXODUS 30:1-10; 37:25-28

THERE are some similarities between the incense altar (sometimes called the "golden altar"), and the altar of burnt offering (sometimes called the "bronze altar"). They both had horns, and provision for being carried by poles passing through four rings set in the four corners.

BUT here the similarities end. It was right that the altar for burnt offering should be of bronze, for it was in the outer court where bronze predominated. The incense altar, if it was to share the characteristics of the other furniture in the Holy Place, had to be of gold: and so it was.

30:1-5. They were also very different in size. Where the great bronze altar had to be big to accommodate the animal sacrifices, the incense altar was quite tiny – a little table, one cubit (50 cm) square, and two cubits (1 metre) high. It had "sides" (literally "walls", see KJV margin), not legs, and was covered with gold. As the top is likened to a "roof" (KJV margin), it was like a small "house of prayer". Also associating it with the table of showbread (and with the ark of the covenant in the Most Holy Place), was the "moulding of gold" around the edge, like a crown (KJV). As crowns normally denote rulership, perhaps we are allowed to see those items provided with gold mouldings as explaining something of the character required for divine rulership: perfect obedience (the showbread), perfect praise (the incense), and perfect reflection of God's nature (the ark of the covenant).

Even though the altar was so small, and could have been carried without the need for carrying poles, in order that the whole process could be dignified and respectful, it was provided with the same method used for all the larger items. The rings and the poles were all covered with gold.

The altar of burnt offering, the incense altar and the table of showbread were all made from acacia wood. The altar of burnt offering was different from the others because it was covered in bronze, while they were covered in gold. As we progress nearer to God, approaching Him in accordance with the demands He has imposed, we recognise the need for a covering for our sinful state. This was provided perfectly by Jesus, through his death and resurrection. In baptism believers "put on" Christ (Galatians 3:27) and benefit from the forgiveness of repented sins as a result of their relationship with him. Finally, when he returns to set up God's kingdom on earth, he will sit in judgement. Those who are accepted by him when he comes, though corruptible now, will "put on incorruption", and though mortal now will "put on immortality" (1 Corinthians 15:54). So it is like our bronze, sinful state being changed into a perfect, pure golden state, fit to stand in the presence of God.

Verse 6. Entering through the doorway into the Holy Place it would be possible to see the table of showbread on the right (or northern) side, and the lampstand on the left (or southern) side. Straight ahead, and right "before the veil", was the altar of incense. There was nowhere else in that part of the tabernacle that was closer to "the ark of the testimony ... the mercy seat" where God has said He would meet with His people.

Verses 7-9. Part of the High Priest's job was to look after the lamps and burn incense on the golden altar. He had to attend to them twice a day, in the morning and in the evening. After dealing with the lamps in the morning (when he dressed and trimmed them), he had to burn incense; and when he went in the evening when the oil in the lamps was replenished, he also had to burn incense. The role of the Altar of Incense on the Day of Atonement is explained on page 54.

The altar of prayer

As our day should begin and end with prayer, so the Israelites' day was marked out by the high priest offering incense to God on their behalf. "In the morning I will direct (my prayer) to you, and I will look up", the Psalmist wrote (5:3), as he did also of the need to commit our ways to God throughout the day and in the evening (31:5). The fragrant incense, specially prepared to a formula to be used only on this altar, and only by the High Priest, anticipated acceptance by God of the nation's prayers. Now, through Christ, believers are assured that their prayers will be heard at all times.

The altar was dedicated to offering this special incense. "No strange incense" should be burnt on it, nor any other sacrifice, whether a "burnt sacrifice", a "grain offering" or a "drink offering". Our prayers are also to be dedicated only to God Himself, and should not ask for anything that does not accord with His purpose.

If the incense altar was an altar, where was the fire? The Exodus record does not explain exactly how it was to be used, but in the priestly instructions in the book of the Levites (Leviticus) we are told that the High Priest took burning coals from the bronze altar in a censer and carried them into the Holy Place. The censer would be like a bowl, probably with chains or a handle attached to carry it with. Once in the Holy Place, the censer could be set down on the altar, the finely ground incense was sprinkled on the red hot coals, and a highly aromatic cloud of smoke was produced, rising up to the ceiling of the tent.

Verse 10. In addition to the daily offerings on the incense altar, once every year, on the day when the High Priest entered the Most Holy Place, he also carried out a special dedication of the golden altar. He placed blood from the sacrifice of atonement on the horns of the altar. Blood was used throughout the tabernacle for cleansing, and it was a way of showing that the altar was set apart for its special purpose, associated with the process of bringing men and women closer to God.

Today we find blood to be the opposite of cleansing. It stains easily, and is almost impossible to remove. But it was used under God's commands to teach of the ultimate cleansing that cannot be reversed. So Jesus' sacrifice is described in the New Testament as "the *precious* blood of Christ" (1 Peter 1:19).

In this way, our consideration of the items placed in the "first tabernacle" leads us to the presence of God. All that stood between the incense altar and the ark of the covenant was the veil, hiding from view the Most Holy Place, the mercy seat and the glory of God.

TEST YOURSELF

1. The incense altar had a "moulding of gold" around it. What other items in the tabernacle also had them?
2. Why was the incense altar placed by the veil?
3. Who could offer incense on the altar?
4. What did the offering represent?
5. How often were the offerings made?
6. What does it teach us about prayer?

For answers turn to page 71.

CHAPTER 15

The veil

EXODUS 26:31,32; 36:35,36

SEPARATING the Holy Place from the Most Holy Place was the curtain known as the veil. As the Holy Place stood for mortal service, with its constant daily reminder of ceaseless toil, and the Most Holy Place represented immortal service, entered by the High Priest only once (each year), the veil represents that which separates us from full communion with God.

WHEN Adam sinned and brought disgrace on the human race, he bore within his body – and passed to all his descendants – a continual reminder of what had happened to him because he had sinned. God punished him by fulfilling His word, for disobedient Adam became a dying creature. But what had caused him to die also operated as a physical principle in him and all his descendants. His body, dying as a result of sin, also bore a bias towards sin. All Adam's descendants sinned.

So long as this situation continued, men and women would be barred from true and perfect fellowship with God. If this could be removed, the last barrier between God and man, erected because of man's sin, could be taken away. Men had proved themselves incapable of doing perfectly all that God asked, so He provided His Son to do what all men had failed to achieve. As one of Adam's descendants, Jesus also bore the same nature. He was a dying creature, and was tempted by the same things and in the same way as all other men. But unlike all other men, he never succumbed to a single temptation. By his total submission to God's commands, and finally by vanquishing the principle of sin when he died in obedience to God's command, he removed the barrier for himself and all who would share his victory. In recognition of this the Gospel writers carefully record that when Jesus died "the veil of the temple was torn in two" (Matthew 27:51).

The veil in the tabernacle should therefore teach us about how we can overcome sin and take hold of what Jesus has achieved for his followers. It should not be seen as a barrier, but as the final clue to how we can properly approach to God and stand in His presence.

26:31. There are similarities between the description of the veil and other woven curtains used in the tabernacle. The descriptions of

THE CHERUBIM

It is appropriate, having found descriptions of various items decorated with the figures of cherubim, to discuss what the cherubim were, and what they represent. They are introduced at the stage in the record when Adam and Eve were barred from the garden of Eden, and more particularly from access to the tree of life.

Cherubim were "placed" at the east of the garden to protect the Tree. The word "placed" literally means "tabernacled". It is therefore possible to see that in an embryo form the tabernacle existed right back in those early days. Most of the things in the tabernacle Moses was instructed to build, were there at that time. There had been a sacrifice so that Adam and Eve could be provided with coats of skins; there was a tree of life, possibly looking like the lampstand; and God's glory in "flaming sword" was also there.

The cherubim were put in Eden by God to "guard the way of the tree of life". They were *guarding* the tree from illicit access by Adam and Eve, but they were also *preserving* the Way to it for all future generations. It is no coincidence that the early Christian believers said that they were following "the Way" (Acts 9:2).

The flaming sword of God's glory "turned every way", flashing and glorious in its splendour. This aspect of the cherubim's work is expanded on the next occasion they appear in the Bible (other than by representation in the tabernacle and the temple). In vision Ezekiel saw cherubim. It was an amazing sight, almost impossible to describe. They were somehow on wheels that allowed them to go in any direction, but it was always "straight ahead".

When they are described in the poetic books, they are likened to God's chariots (see Psalm 18:10). Their name means those who are grasped or held tightly, so closely associated are they with God's purpose. In Ezekiel's vision they also had four faces; all expressing different characteristics.

From this information we can conclude that the cherubim are those who do God's will perfectly, who are driven by Him, and by a desire to serve Him: "Wherever the spirit wanted to go, they went" (Ezekiel 1:20). The characteristics revealed about them should be the aim of all disciples.

the first covering for the tabernacle, of the curtain for the door to the Holy Place, and of the gateway to the outer court all mention fine linen thread, blue, purple, and scarlet. On the veil and on the first covering we are specifically told that the decoration was based on the cherubim. Though the material and colours were the same on the curtains used for the gate and doorway, cherubim are not mentioned. The theme may have continued, but it would be more appropriate if the decoration on the outer hangings only hinted at what could be seen by anyone privileged to enter into the tabernacle.

On the "fine linen", the figures of the cherubim were worked with "cunning work" in "blue, and purple, and scarlet". Passages elsewhere in the Bible provide information that explains what cherubim represent. See box alongside.

It is possible now to understand why cherubim are used so often in the tabernacle. If the purpose of the tabernacle was to teach the Israelites how they should fit themselves to be holy like their God, the same lesson had already commenced with the cherubim.

Verse 32. Though the door to the tabernacle was hung from five pillars, the veil, which was about the same size, was hung from only four.

We have seen that the cherubim had four faces, so the supporting pillars emphasised these characteristics. The foursquare camp, finally reflecting the foursquare Most Holy Place, was also a symbol of the cherubim. If Israel had only appreciated how they could have been God's chariot, driven by Him, their history would have been different.

The few occasions when they did (notably when they faithfully took the walled city of Jericho under the guidance of Joshua) showed what could have been accomplished if only they had submitted totally to God's will.

The same is true for us today. How easy it is to rely on our own abilities and strengths, and call on God only when things are difficult, or when we feel unable to succeed in the ways we want.

The four pillars were of gold, like the five pillars at the entrance. But while those stood on bronze bases, the pillars supporting the veil were on silver ones. Under stringent conditions mortal beings could enter the Holy Place; only redeemed ones could enter the Most Holy Place.

The lessons of the veil were taught to Jacob when he was fleeing from his angry brother Esau. As he lay down to sleep he dreamed of a ladder between earth and heaven, the communication between God and men. Angels were ascending and descending on it. What he said when he awoke is very appropriate to the *tabernacle* and the *veil*:

> "This is none other than the house of God, and this is the gate of heaven."
>
> (Genesis 28:17)

TEST YOURSELF

1. What other article in the tabernacle was made and decorated like the veil?
2. Why was the use of cherubim appropriate?
3. Where are cherubim first mentioned in the Bible?
4. What conditions are necessary to pass through the veil?
5. What, simply, does the veil then represent?

For answers turn to page 71.

CHAPTER 16

The Most Holy Place

AFTER all the preliminary parts, entering the Most Holy Place was to enter into the very presence of God Himself. How could the Israelites have understood anything else about this remarkable central portion of the tabernacle?

IT was a simple cube, where the Holy Place was a double cube. Ten cubits was the measure of all its dimensions (5 metres long, wide and high). Three walls were of pure gold, reflecting the intricate pattern on the veil. But in order that there can be a reflection there has to be a source of light. The Holy Place was illuminated by the lampstand, but there was no physical provision for light in the Most Holy Place. Though no-one regularly went into the Most Holy Place, it cannot be imagined there would never be a need for light there. The answer is found in the vision of the new Jerusalem given by revelation to the Apostle John exiled on the island of Patmos.

In the city of New Jerusalem:

"Its length and breadth and height are equal ... And the city had no need of the sun or of the moon to shine in it, for the glory of God illuminated it, and the Lamb is its light."
(Revelation 21:16,23)

So also in the Most Holy Place, the glory of God, who chose to dwell among His people, provided the light: "You who dwell between the cherubim, shine forth!" (Psalm 80:1). His presence was also marked by the cloudy pillar that had led the Israelites out from Egypt. It protected them from the threat of the Egyptian troops, and in the wilderness acted as a shelter from the burning sun. At night time the pillar of cloud was like a glowing fire, so awe-inspiring is God's glory.

Because the presence of God dwelt there, the Most Holy Place was a representation on earth of heaven itself. Everything about it was pure: its dimensions, its materials, and its design. Purity was demanded also on the one occasion every year when a representative of the nation was allowed to enter.

Every other day of the year Aaron was dressed in colourful robes, themselves able to teach important lessons about Godly things, but on one special day every year these magnificent robes had to be removed and replaced by a simple, plain white robe. In the change of clothes was marked the change from his function of representing God to men, to a position where he represented men, sanctified by the sacrifices, to God.

The one day was called "The Day of Atonement" and looked forward to the time when men's sins would finally be forgiven and their natures changed so that God and man can peacefully co-exist. In contrast to the rest of the service of the tabernacle, which was required day in and day out, the Day of Atonement taught the Israelites that a change to immortality can only occur once, as a result of the "one sacrifice for sins *for ever*".

On this one day each year, the Most Holy Place had another item of furniture associated with it. In the Letter to the Hebrews we read: "The Holiest of all ... had the golden censer, and the ark of the covenant" (9:4, KJV). This censer was "full of burning coals of fire from the altar" (Leviticus 16:12). Every other day incense was offered on the incense altar in the Holy Place. But on the Day of Atonement the High Priest offered it in the Most Holy Place, so "that the cloud of the incense may cover the mercy seat ... lest he die" (Leviticus 16:13). When Solomon's Temple is described (a larger and non-portable version of the tabernacle), it is noted of the incense altar that it "*belonged to*" the Most Holy Place (1 Kings 6:22, RV), fulfilling its true role on the Day of Atonement.

During the wilderness journey, there may have been occasions in addition to the Day of Atonement when someone else went in. God said to Moses:

> "There I will meet with you, and I will speak with you from above the mercy seat ... of all things which I will give you in commandment to the children of Israel." (Exodus 25:22)

Because God *spoke* from the Most Holy Place it was called "the oracle".

Despite the great value of the materials used in the tabernacle, and the exquisite workmanship involved, this sanctuary was extremely simple. God has never required great pomp and show, nor does He wish men to complicate the beautiful simplicity of His teachings. He wants men and women with willing hearts to serve Him faithfully, believe in the work of His Son the Lord Jesus Christ, and attempt to follow his example in all things. Only in this way can God really dwell amongst His people, in hearts that are prepared to welcome Him.

TEST YOURSELF

1. How did the shape of the Most Holy Place differ from the Holy Place?
2. How was it lit?
3. Who was allowed to enter the Most Holy Place?
4. Ultimately, what does the Most Holy Place represent?

For answers turn to page 72.

TEST YOURSELF

1. Was there anything other than the ark in the Most Holy Place?
2. Why was the wood completely covered in the construction of the ark?
3. Why were the carrying poles not removed from the ark when it was placed in the sanctuary?
4. Why was the ark called the "ark of the testimony"?
5. What did the testimony witness to?

For answers turn to page 72.

CHAPTER 17

The Ark of the Covenant

EXODUS 25:10-16; 37:1-5

INSIDE the Most Holy Place there was only one item of furniture. Though the room itself was not very large, this item did not fill it. The room was 5 metres long, 5 metres wide, and 5 metres high. The piece of furniture was only 1.2 metres long, 75 cm wide and 75 cm high, about the size of a small dining table. But it was not a table, it was more like a box, made from wood covered with pure gold.

IT was called an ark, like the vessel God used to save Noah and his family from the worldwide flood that destroyed the wickedness of men in his day. Moses himself had been saved by water in an ark, for when he was a very young baby his parents placed him in an ark made from bulrushes and put it on the waters of the river to save him from being captured and killed by the Egyptians. Both those arks were vessels of *salvation*, so it is not surprising that this one was too.

25:10-15. Other articles in the tabernacle were made from acacia wood covered with gold, but only the ark was covered with gold "inside and out" so that no wood could be seen. Around the upper edge was "a moulding of gold", like the ones on the table of shewbread and altar of incense. Also, like other articles made for the tabernacle, the ark was provided with means to carry it when the camp moved on in its journey.

"Four rings of gold" were fitted to the four corners, two rings on each side. Through them were passed wooden poles covered with gold. Only in connection with the ark was the commandment given that the poles "shall be in the rings of the ark: they *shall not be taken from it*". Symbolising the presence of God in their midst, the ark was always ready to move so that God and His people would not be separated.

Verse 16. The ark was basically a container for various items. Principally it was to hold "the testimony", the two stone tables inscribed with the Ten Commandments. These commandments were a testimony (or witness) of what God wanted men and women to do, so that they would be without excuse. In addition, and at a later stage, other items were placed there to witness to significant events. Aaron's rod was put there to show that the priesthood was to be in his family, and so was a golden pot containing manna, commemorating God's gracious care of the children of Israel while they wandered through the desert.

CHAPTER 18

The Mercy Seat

EXODUS 25:17-22; 37:6-9

THE ark, the golden container of the tables of the testimony, also had a lid. It differed from the rest of the ark, which was made from acacia wood covered with gold. Like the lampstand, the lid was made only of pure gold. It was big enough to fit completely over the ark (1.2 metres long × 75 cm wide) and had, constructed in one piece with it, two figures of cherubim.

25:17,18. The cover expressed the outstanding characteristic of Israel's God – His mercy. This quality is shown most clearly in His provision "to cover" man's sin. God "covered" the sin in Eden by making coats of skins, showing the importance of sacrifice. He "covers" believers' sins through the "merciful" sacrifice of His Son, the Lord Jesus Christ. This provision was foretold by the mercy seat in the Most Holy Place. The idea of covering is brought out in the NIV translation where the mercy seat is called an "atonement cover".

One cherub was at each end looking inwards, with wings covering the golden lid, and sheltering it. Also like the lampstand, the cherubim were made of "hammered work". The qualities they represent must be formed in men and women over a period of time, moulded by the events of life which can become a discipline for good, or a temptation to do evil.

Both the Holy Place and the Most Holy Place therefore had one item of furnishing made wholly from pure gold. This teaches that the vitally important way of learning about God in this life (the times represented by the Holy Place) is from His word: the lamp to our feet and light to our path.

Verses 19,20. Though we have learned that cherubim have four faces, and in Ezekiel's vision it seems that each face looked in a different direction, on the ark they were focused on the centre of the lid. This seems a strange thing until we read that the lid was more than a cover to the ark: it was really God's throne. Called "the mercy seat", it showed His most wonderful characteristic. When He was described to Moses it was the quality of mercy that was emphasised:

> "The LORD, the LORD God, merciful and gracious, long-suffering, and abounding in goodness and truth." (Exodus 34:6)

So the space above the mercy seat, guarded (as in Genesis 3:24) by the cherubim, was where

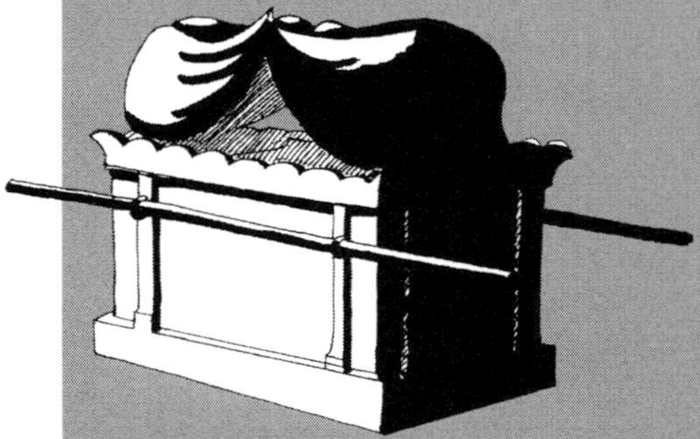

the glory of God dwelt. From here His light would illuminate the Most Holy Place, and from here also He would give the commandments to Moses for the good of the nation.

Throughout the rest of the tabernacle, the faithful Israelite was being led to a contemplation of God and His holiness. In the mercy seat He found it fully explained: everything centred upon this holy provision.

An empty space

But there was nothing there! The religions of the nations around Israel all had their idols, representations of weird figures conjured up by warped minds. The Israelites had been warned not to make "any carved image, or any likeness of anything ... you shalt not bow down to them or serve them" (Exodus 20:3,4). Even though the tabernacle was a wonderfully constructed, and carefully crafted sanctuary, it was not to become an object of worship in itself. The God of Israel could not be represented by anything man-made, so when we reach the place where He chose to dwell, there is nothing there.

This was the mistake Israel and the Philistines made when the ark of God was brought among the battle lines in the days when Samuel was young.

The Israelites thought "it" could save them out of the hand of their enemies (1 Samuel 4:3). The Philistines were afraid, and said, "God is come into the camp" (verse 7). Both were wrong. The precious things of God cannot be used as "magic charms" the way Israel treated the ark, nor can God be contained in anything made by man, as Solomon declared: "Heaven and the heaven of heavens cannot contain you. How much less this temple which I have built?" (1 Kings 8:27).

But when Aaron went in as he was commanded to do, the whole place was filled with God's glory, like a cloud. Aaron knew His glory was there, and was aware of His Holy presence.

Verses 21,22. The relationship of all the parts is crucial to an understanding of what God intended the central part of His sanctuary to teach the Israelites. The mercy seat had to cover the ark, and the ark contained the testimony – God's law for the people. That law was to prove impossible for sinful man to keep, yet God is gracious and abundant in goodness and truth. So over ("above and on") the ark and the testimony was His throne of mercy. As the Psalmist said: "If you, LORD, should mark iniquities ... who could stand? But there is forgiveness with you, that you may be feared" (130:3,4).

May the tabernacle be the means of us discovering this great Truth, and choosing to serve God with willing hearts, trying to show forth His characteristics of goodness, mercy and truth despite the evil that surrounds us.

TEST YOURSELF

1. What material was the mercy seat made from?
2. What other item in the tabernacle was made from the same material?
3. What was the difference between the cherubim Ezekiel saw in vision (Ezekiel 1), and the two cherubim on the mercy seat?
4. What was between the cherubim?
5. The mercy seat was the central part of the whole tabernacle. What does this teach us about our own lives?

For answers turn to page 72.

CHAPTER 19

Setting up the tabernacle

EXODUS 40:1-11,17-33

THE intricate details of how the tabernacle and all its furniture was to be made was not the end of the specific commands from God in relation to His sanctuary. It was just as important to ensure that His commands were followed when the tabernacle was erected, and when it was taken down.

AS with the description of how the tabernacle was to be made, so the description about its erection is repeated. The first time explains how it was to be done; the second time records the first occasion when these commands were carried out.

40:2. Once the various component parts of the tabernacle had all been completed, it was ready to be fitted together. To show that it would mark the start of a new arrangement, this was to be done "on the first day of the month". Just before God brought the Israelites out from Egypt, He had declared: "This month shall be your beginning of months" (Exodus 12:2). So from that time onwards, the month Abib, the month when the Passover was celebrated, was to be the beginning of their sacred calendar. By first setting up the tabernacle in the month when the Passover was celebrated, God's redemption and the promise of His continual and abiding presence were shown to be closely related.

The day the tabernacle was set up was the first day of the second full year in the wilderness (verse 17). Thus, it had taken most of the first year to prepare and fashion all the different parts.

Verses 3-8. The first job was to put up the tent, with its coverings. Once that was done, the ark of the covenant, covered by the veil, could be placed inside. As the central feature in the tabernacle, it was fitting that this was the first thing to be put in its place. But it could not be uncovered before all the other items had been carefully positioned. The order to be followed was:

- The table of showbread, with the bread and its utensils;
- The lampstand, with its lamps lit;
- The golden incense altar; and
- The hanging for the door.

Outside the tabernacle, and still working from the centre outwards, the next items to be set in place were the bronze altar of burnt offering, and the laver. The laver had to be filled with water.

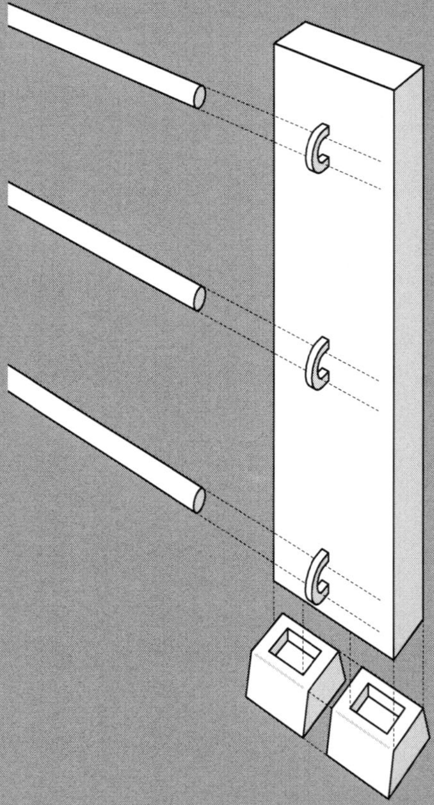

Only when all these things were done was the fabric fence hung up around the courtyard, and finally "the hanging at the court gate" completed the task.

Verses 9-11. Before the tabernacle could be used as a centre for the Israelites' sacrifices, and for their worship of God, it had to be dedicated for the work. Throughout this chapter it seems that Moses is the one who carried out the work. It is not possible to say whether he only did it on the first occasion the tabernacle was erected, whether he was involved at other times as well, or whether he repeated the commands given to him by God, and the work was really carried out by Aaron and his sons. In very many ways Moses foreshadowed the work of Jesus, and it would therefore be fitting for him to set up the tabernacle only on the first occasion, just as Jesus completed his work on earth and does not need to repeat it.

Even though we may not know for certain who it was that actually performed the tasks, each item in the tabernacle, together with all the furnishings, was anointed with the holy anointing oil. From the second description (verses 17-33) it seems that this was done as each stage was completed. The anointing was to show that the tabernacle was dedicated to the worship of God, and would not be used for anything else. God demands the same dedication today from those who wish to approach Him. Every part of our lives can similarly be devoted to Him.

Verses 12-15. At the same time, Moses was told to wash and anoint Aaron and his sons, so that they would be able to serve in the tabernacle as priests. Their priesthood was to be "everlasting ... throughout their generations". In the Bible, "everlasting" does not always mean "for ever"; it sometimes relates to a set period of time, an age, or as we might say, an era. We know that Aaron's priesthood was limited, because there is another who is a "priest *for ever* after the order of Melchisedek" (see Hebrews 6:20), a priestly order established before Aaron's and which would outlast his.

The anointing of the tabernacle, everything in it, and all those whose job it would be to serve in it, clearly showed how it was different from anything man could have fashioned out of his own thoughts. The tabernacle and its offerings were all designed by God, and He gave the pattern to Moses when he received the Law from God in the mountain of Sinai.

Verse 16. Moses was truly a servant of God's, for, "according to all that the Lord commanded him, so he did". Later in the chapter it is put even more simply: "So Moses finished the work" (verse 33). The project was ambitious. The Israelites were a nation without a country. They escaped the Egyptians, only to find themselves in an inhospitable wilderness. Just like we would have reacted, they started to complain, and to think that they would have been better staying in Egypt as slaves. As Moses was prepared for his job of leadership during his forty years in the wilderness of Midian (Exodus chapters 3 and 4), so Israel would be prepared as a nation during another forty years of wilderness life. In this period of preparation, the tabernacle was an important, and ever-present witness to what God wanted them to do. Setting up the tabernacle was, therefore, a little like starting to establish the nation.

TEST YOURSELF

1. Once the tabernacle was erected, what was the first item to be placed inside?
2. After everything had finally been positioned, what needed to be done before the tabernacle could be used?
3. What does anointing signify?
4. Aaron and his sons were to be the priests for Israel. What other priesthood is mentioned in the Bible?
5. Who is priest now for God's people?

For answers turn to page 73.

CHAPTER 20

The tabernacle on the move

NUMBERS 4

THE careful arrangements that directed how the tabernacle was to be set up also applied whenever the camp was moved. The ark, symbolising the presence of God in the midst of the nation, led the whole camp to its new site. Each other section of the tabernacle had specific regulations concerning how and when it could be moved.

AS with all other aspects of the service of the tabernacle, Aaron and his sons were central to the details of dismantling, and packing. But when the tabernacle was ready for transporting to a new location, the Kohathite family was responsible.

4:5,6. The first job was to cover the ark with the veil, then with a badger skin covering, and finally with a cloth, "entirely of blue". As we have seen (page 21), the use of blue in the tabernacle fabrics was a representation of things to do with God.

Different coloured cloths were used when the tabernacle was being dismantled. Some articles, like the ark, were covered by a blue cloth; others by a purple cloth; and some by a red cloth.

Some of the items of furniture had at this stage to have carrying poles fitted to them ready for the journey. The ark was unique in this respect. Its carrying poles were always in place, showing that God is ever ready to move with His people.

Of all the separate items in the tabernacle, only the ark of the testimony had the blue cloth visible as the people journeyed. For everything else, the final covering was made from skins. In every Bible passage that deals with the tabernacle, a distinction is made between the "ark of [God's] strength" (Psalm 132:8) and the other items that show how He should be approached. This distinction was openly declared when the nation was on the move.

Verses 7,8. The next item to be covered was "the table of showbread". A blue cloth was placed over this before the various instruments associated with the table, and the showbread itself, were replaced. Over the whole lot (table, blue cloth, dishes, etc., and bread) was spread "a scarlet cloth", and over that "a covering of badger skins". Quite carefully, a distinction was being made between the table (covered with blue), representing God, and the bread showing the life of the people (covered with red, representative of sin). The covering of skins showed that sinful man and God can only associate on the basis of sacrifice: a lesson taught first to Adam and Eve after they had sinned (Genesis 3:21).

Verses 9-11. The lampstand was the next item to be prepared for carrying. It, and all its fittings, were covered with a blue cloth, and then with badgers' skins before being placed on a plank so that the weight could be shared between at least two people.

The tiny incense altar was similarly covered, first with a blue cloth and then with badgers' skins. As it had its own carrying poles, it did not need any separate arrangement for transportation.

Verses 12-14. Any other "utensils of service" were placed together inside a blue cloth, covered by badgers' skins and placed on a plank for carrying. What were not included in this bundle were the instruments associated with the altar of burnt offering. Those, and the altar itself, were dealt with differently.

First, the ashes from the fire were removed, and the altar was covered with "a purple cloth". When the colour purple occurs in the tabernacle, it is associated with the saving work of Jesus. The one sacrifice Jesus offered for sins was shown to be necessary by the regular daily offerings burnt on the great bronze altar.

Onto the purple cloth were placed all the various other instruments: "censers, fleshhooks, shovels, basons, and vessels", before a badger skin covering was thrown over them all. Like the ark, the table of showbread, and the incense altar, the altar of burnt offering had its own carrying poles. These were put in place ready for when the camp set out on its journey.

One item, not mentioned in this passage, was the laver. During the time the tabernacle was being moved the laver could be seen by all the Israelites. It was a silent witness to the salvation always available from God (see page 31).

Verse 15. Only Aaron and his sons could be involved in this work, because it was dealing with things which were "holy". They were specially selected and prepared to deal with the holy things, and the emphasis this gave should have taught the Israelites of the care God requires in any approach that is made to Him, and of the preparation of Jesus, through whom alone we can now draw near to God.

The Kohathites were warned not to touch any of these holy things, "lest they die". This was like the punishment in store for Adam if he disobeyed the commandment concerning the tree of the knowledge of good and evil. It was equally severe and as certain of fulfilment. Later in Israel's history, inhabitants of a Kohathite town disobeyed the commandment, and were immediately smitten by God (see 1 Samuel 6:19).

How did Israel know when to journey?

The children of Israel wandered in the wilderness as a punishment for their unfaithfulness. The small advance party sent by Moses to search out the land brought back such a depressing message of the difficulties to be faced by any attacking force that the people decided they could not attempt it. Of the twelve men who were sent, only Joshua and Caleb recognised that with the hand of God to assist them the Land could be theirs.

God's punishment was to lead them about in the wilderness until all that unfaithful generation died. Their journeyings were therefore not their own decision, but God's. The instructions were simple. The great cloud, which was a continual reminder of God's abiding presence, normally rested over the tabernacle, presumably centred upon the position where the ark of the testimony was sited. So long as the cloud remained in that position, the camp was to stay where it was: "Whether it was two days, a month, or a year that the cloud remained above the tabernacle, the children of Israel would remain encamped, and not journey" (Numbers 9:22).

"When the cloud was taken up from above the tabernacle, the children of Israel went onward in all their journeys" (Exodus 40:36). In this aspect of their life, God totally regulated their actions.

All of mankind needs to learn that God's commandments should be kept. The children of Israel were not free to move just when they wanted to, if they were going to be truly the people of God. Should not we try to learn the same lesson, living our lives more in harmony with His will?

TEST YOURSELF

1. As the nation journeyed, which item of furniture could be distinguished from all the others?
2. What was the essential difference between the blue covering and the covering of skins?
3. Aaron and his sons were responsible for preparing the tabernacle furniture to be carried. Who were responsible for carrying it?
4. When items of furniture had no carrying poles, how were they transported?
5. What did God command those who transported the tabernacle furniture *not* to do?

For answers turn to page 73.

Outline answers to questions

SOME of the questions in the text are straightforward ones, designed to help you test how well you have absorbed the information in each section. Others attempt to extend the information, asking you to apply the principles of the tabernacle to the sort of life believers in Christ should try to live.

If you can answer most of the questions more or less correctly you are ready to go on to the next section. If you feel you have not done well, it is worth reading through the section again before moving on, looking up the scriptural passages. Then try assessing yourself again!

Chapter 01 – "A closer look"

THE CAMP OF ISRAEL – PAGE 7

1. In the middle of the encampment there was a clear space free from the living tents of the Israelites. The tabernacle was erected in the centre of this open area.
2. Though all the other tribes had space allocated for their tents among the general area away from the centre, members of the tribe of Levi were allowed to pitch their tents immediately around where the tabernacle was sited.
3. The rich and costly materials needed to make the tabernacle could not be found in the wilderness of Sinai; they had been forced into the Israelites' hands by the Egyptians just before Moses led the people out of slavery.
4. A sanctuary is a place set apart, specially kept for the worship of God.
5. God had shown His presence among the Israelites by a pillar of cloud in the daytime, seen at night time as a pillar of fire. When the tabernacle was constructed and the ark placed in it, the pillar of cloud rested on the tabernacle, right over the Most Holy Place.
6. The priests' job was to present the sacrifices to God that were brought by the faithful Israelites. They thus stood in place of God, especially the High Priest. The special clothing that they had, and the lessons it was able to teach, showed the rest of the nation that God is holy and righteous and true.
7. The lesson for individuals today is basically the same as for the nation of Israel in Moses' day. God should be at the centre of the believer's life, so that everything is done with an awareness of His close presence. In this way His Name and purpose will be upheld

and honoured. The greatest example of this devotion was provided by the Lord Jesus Christ, whose saving work can be seen, foreshadowed in the various aspects of the tabernacle.

8. Only you can answer this!

THE TABERNACLE AND ITS PARTS – PAGE 9

1. Any Israelite, wishing to make an offering to God as provided in the Law given through Moses, could go to the door of the tabernacle. But the service of the tabernacle was reserved for the priests only, those who were members of the tribe of Levi.
2. Though it was the centre of worship for the whole nation of Israel, the site of the tabernacle was quite small. A space only half the length and half the width of a football pitch was needed to erect it on.
3. The great bronze (brasen) altar, and the laver, also made from bronze.
4. The altar was used for the sacrifice that needed to be offered to God, as He had commanded. The laver contained water. The priests had to wash themselves before *and after* every action of service in the tabernacle.
5. Only the priests could prepare and offer the sacrifices, and only the priests could use the water from the laver.

PAGE 11

1. Despite the luxurious richness of the materials and design of the tabernacle, the floor was the desert earth.
2. Man was made in the beginning from the dust of the earth. All the elements man is made from are the common elements of all matter, and the beaten earth floor of the tabernacle would remind the Israelites of this. But man's life comes from God. God breathed into Adam's nostrils the breath of life, and man became a living being. Man's very existence is thus dependant on God's grace. He has declared the only way that man can be saved from returning to the ground. This "Way of Salvation" was shown in the different parts of the tabernacle, and through the later work of Jesus.
3. The tabernacle was divided into two parts. The first was called the Holy Place, and the second was the Most Holy Place.
4. The furniture in the Holy Place consisted of the lampstand, the table of shewbread, and the altar of incense.
5. As the inside of the tabernacle would have been very dark, the seven-branched lampstand provided the light in the Holy Place. But there was no artificial light in the Most Holy Place. It was lit by the glory of God's presence, shining from above the mercy seat and between the cherubim.

6. The main contents of the ark of the testimony were the two tables of stone containing the Ten Commandments, summarising the Law. During the wilderness journey, Aaron's rod was added, and also a jar containing an incorruptible sample of the manna God had sent to provide food for the travelling Israelites.
7. The covering for the ark was called the mercy seat. It was made wholly of gold, and had the figures of two cherubim formed, one at each end, and looking inwards towards where the glory of God would dwell.

Chapter 03 – "The purpose of the tabernacle"

PAGE 18

1. The real ruler of Israel was God. As He said to Samuel when the people in his day asked for a king to lead them into battle, so that they could be like the other nations around, "they have not rejected thee, but they have rejected me, that I should not reign over them" (1 Samuel 8:7).
2. The key word in this section is "willingly". Although God could have made a race of robots, perfectly performing His will, what He wants is for men and women, of their own free will, to choose to serve Him because they recognise Him as their God and Saviour.
3. God can only be approached on the basis He has declared. Since the times of Jesus this has meant that "there is no other name under heaven given among men, by which we must be saved" (Acts 4:12). The tabernacle shows this by teaching about sacrifice, baptism, prayer and devotion.
4. The tabernacle was a pattern of God's great plan of salvation centred in Jesus, and is able to teach in a memorable way some of the profound truths about it.
5. Believers today, like the Israelites of old, have been redeemed from worldly Egypt and from the bondage to sin, and are journeying to the promised kingdom. God promises, through Christ, to be with His followers now, just as He was with the nation in their wilderness wanderings. His protection and care are never failing, so long as He is approached in the way He has demanded.

Chapter 04 – "The materials and craftsmen"

PAGE 23

1. Standing between bronze and gold, between red and blue, the silver and purple linked those things representing sinful man, and those representing the holy God. Only Jesus, who was born sharing man's nature, has lived a wholly sinless life, and can therefore enter into a full understanding of man's difficulties while at the same time upholding God's holiness.

2. The pure and precious gold, and the heavenly blue, were fitting representations of God Himself, and of heaven, where He dwells.
3. To show that ultimately everything belongs to God, there was a special provision in the law for "buying back" from Him, animals, children, etc. This process is known as "redemption". For the redemption of people, a special silver coin was used, and this regular payment should have shown the Israelites their need for redemption from sin. This need was met by Jesus, who paid the redemption price for all believers.
4. The coverings for the tabernacle helped to hide the interior from view, and protected it from the effects of the weather.
5. Gold is one of the most precious materials in the world. In the Bible it is used to show the quality of tried and perfected faith, something that can only be fully achieved when man is in an immortal state. It is therefore fitting that this metal should be used in the tabernacle in association with those things that are closely connected with the presence of God Himself.

Chapter 05 – "The outer court"

PAGE 26

1. The tabernacle was separated from the main camp of the Israelites to show the holiness of God, and the need for mortal men and women to prepare and sanctify themselves before approaching Him.
2. Holy means "separate", or "set apart".
3. Bronze (or brass) was the metal most used in the outer court.
4. Though the courtyard tells us a lot about man and his basic sinfulness, there are elements that teach about how God has planned for man's salvation. The redemptive work of Christ is shown by the silver fittings for the surrounding fence to be an essential part of this plan.
5. God has revealed that He will only be approached in the way He has appointed.
6. Only the priests involved with the service of the tabernacle were allowed into the outer courtyard.

Chapter 06 – "The altar of burnt offering"

PAGE 28

1. Altars were not to be made of hewn stones, nor to be raised up from the ground so that they could only be approached by steps. Both of these things would have been attractive to man's pride, so God specifically said they should not be associated with His worship.
2. The sacrifices required under the Law were brought by individual Israelites to be offered on the altar by the priests, but on their behalf.

3. The priests' food was provided from parts of some of the sacrifices, but essentially the sacrifice was God's food. The reason the sacrifice was offered – because the offerer recognised his need for forgiveness, and wished to honour his God – was pleasing to God, as food is pleasing to us.
4. There was a grating provided in the altar, probably to support the fire and allow the air to circulate beneath it.
5. Like all of the tabernacle, the altar needed to be transported around the wilderness as the Israelites travelled from place to place. Carrying poles and location rings were provided for this purpose.
6. The altar for believers has been provided in the person and work of the Lord Jesus Christ. His life and sacrifice were fully pleasing to God, so all who approach Him through Jesus, in the way He has appointed, can be accepted by Him.

Chapter 07 – "The laver"

PAGE 31

1. The laver was simply a bronze container for water, used ceremonially in connection with the tabernacle service.
2. Only the priests (Aaron's sons) could use it.
3. They washed their hands and their feet before and after each act of service in the tabernacle.
4. The bronze was provided by the women in the camp who brought polished mirrors to be melted down and re-cast into the laver described and shown to Moses by God.
5. The mirrors had previously been used by the women as a cosmetic accessory and, possibly, their vanity was increased. The Bible teaches accurately about the natural state of man, showing the importance of the heart and not the outward appearance. Significantly, it shows the characteristics of God Himself, and of His Son, the Lord Jesus Christ. Believers are asked to pattern their lives on him and attempt to "mirror" their characters on his. Only God's word can give us this information.
6. Only you can answer this!

Chapter 08 – "The structure of the tabernacle"

PAGE 34

1. The instructions for making the tabernacle needed Moses, who was shown a "pattern" when he was in the mountain with God, to explain some of the details. The record has been preserved for us, not so that we can make an exact copy of the tabernacle (the need for that has now passed), but so that we can learn the lessons it should have taught the Israelites about God and His purpose.

2. The carefully designed connections between the various parts of the tabernacle teach us about fellowship and the unity that exists between fellow-believers, God, and the Lord Jesus Christ.
3. In the same way, the human body is made up of various parts, having different functions, but needing every part so that it can operate properly.
4. All the boards in the tabernacle were similar, showing there is no distinction between believers, "for ye are all one in Christ Jesus" (Galatians 3:28). Yet each part had its own job to fulfil, and was necessary for the compactness of the whole building. The same is true for members of ecclesias in Christ.
5. Only you can answer this!

Chapter 09 – "The coverings of the tabernacle"

PAGE 38

1. The first curtain was closely associated with the wooden tabernacle structure: indeed, the tabernacle was incomplete without it. The other coverings grouped together were the "tent" which covered the tabernacle.
2. The tabernacle structure (Hebrew, *mishkan*) was God's dwelling place. It was so designed as to show the attributes and characteristics of God and how He wishes men and women to be glorified. The rest of the coverings and the courtyard indicated man's sinfulness, and his need of redemption.
3. The fabric and workmanship of the first covering was like the veil which hung between the Holy Place and the Most Holy Place.
4. Though the descriptions of the tabernacle show that ropes were used to provide stability to the walls, and the coverings would rest on these, there is no information which allows us to be certain how four large and heavy curtains were supported over the roof of the tabernacle.
5. The inner (linen) curtain, and the second (goats' hair) curtain were both made in two parts and connected together by loops and clasps.

Chapter 10 – "The door"

PAGE 40

6. The linen hanging that formed the gateway to the courtyard was very similar to the hanging at the doorway to the Holy Place. They were both embroidered in blue, purple and scarlet, though no indication is given of the design that was fashioned on them. It could have been the same, or it may have been slightly different.

7. Only the priest could enter into the tabernacle through the door. He also had to fulfil certain requirements to show that he was not defiled, otherwise he could not have entered.
8. Jesus described himself as the "door" of the sheepfold – the family of God can be entered only by association with the saving work of Christ.

Chapter 11 – "The Holy Place"

PAGE 41

1. Jesus stands between man and God. As the great High Priest, prayers to God can be offered through him by his disciples. Jesus has been transformed from mortality to immortality, and the promise is made to all his followers that they can share his glory if they remain faithful to his commands.
2. The Holy Place is described in the Letter to the Hebrews as standing for "the time then present" (Hebrews 9:9), i.e. when the Law of Moses was in operation.
3. The need for daily replenishing of the lamps on the lampstand, and the weekly replacement of the loaves on the table of showbread, show that the Israelites and ourselves are still living on an earth cursed by sin. The promise of release has been made certain in Christ, but cannot be fulfilled until the day when those who are truly "in Christ" will be able to "pass through the veil" (mortal flesh) into immortality.

Chapter 12 – "The table of showbread"

PAGE 43

1. In the Bible bread is used as an example of human labour (Genesis 3:19).
2. The twelve loaves represented the whole nation of Israel (made up of twelve tribes).
3. The bread was dedicated to God, and was really His food.
4. It was eaten by the priests after being "on show" for seven days. Only they could eat it, because it was holy (see 1 Samuel 21:4-6).
5. The meal was an act of fellowship. Like believers in Christ sharing in the 'breaking of bread', the priests were in fellowship with God – whose bread it really was.
6. The bread was "on show" before God to demonstrate how the Israelites accepted that they should love Him with "all their heart ... soul ... and mind" (Matthew 22:37). But the bread also "showed" how God wishes to be united with His creation, and how He has purposed this great reunion will be accomplished.

Chapter 13 – "The lampstand"

PAGE 46

1. The Tree of Life in the Garden of Eden, and Aaron's rod that budded.
2. The priests (Aaron and his sons).
3. Pure olive oil was used for the lamps. The olives had to be finely beaten: only the best, rigorously prepared, is good enough in God's service.
4. Jesus – the word made flesh (John 1:141 – described himself as "the light of the world" (John 8:12). The Gospel of salvation is therefore a light for those who now walk in the darkness of the world.

Chapter 14 – "The altar of incense"

PAGE 49

1. Three items of the tabernacle's furniture had decorative crowns around their edges. These were:
   a. The incense altar;
   b. The table of showbread; and
   c. The ark of the testimony.
2. Because prayer is so intimately associated with God and His dwelling place, but is available to those who are living under the constraints of sin and in a defiled world, the altar of incense was placed in the Holy Place, but as near as possible to the veil and ark of the covenant. It formed part of the process that conveyed the people's prayers to God.
3. Only the priests (Aaron and his sons) could offer incense on the golden altar.
4. The incense, producing a sweet-smelling cloud of smoke, represented how prayer is something pleasing to God.
5. Incense was offered daily in connection with the other regular offerings associated with the tabernacle.
6. Like the incense, which was carefully and rigorously prepared, prayers cannot be offered other than as God has demanded.

Chapter 15 – "The veil"

PAGE 52

1. The innermost (first) covering over the tabernacle was also of linen, embroidered with cherubim in scarlet, purple and blue.
2. The cherubim, throughout scripture, are associated with the saving and redemptive work of God. They were beings that reflected His characteristics and were responsive to His ways – just the things God wishes from all men and women.

3. Cherubim are first mentioned when God banished Adam and Eve from the garden and set a guard on the "way of the tree of life" (Genesis 3:24).
4. The veil in the temple was torn in two when Jesus died. This shows that only victory over sin can allow someone to pass through the veil.
5. The veil is therefore fittingly representative of sinful flesh (Hebrews 10:20).

Chapter 16 – "The Most Holy Place"

PAGE 54

1. The Most Holy Place was a perfect cube; its length, breadth and height were all 10 cubits, whereas the Holy Place was the same width and height, but exactly twice the length.
2. The only light in the Most Holy Place came from the glory of God that shone from between the cherubim on the mercy seat over the ark.
3. Only the High Priest was allowed to enter the Most Holy Place, and he could only enter once every year, on the Day of Atonement.
4. All the provisions of the Most Holy Place help to describe God, His character, His ways, and where He is pleased to dwell. He has declared that, though His throne is in heaven, He wishes to be enthroned in the hearts of men and women who will honour His name.

Chapter 17 – "The Ark of the Covenant"

PAGE 55

1. Nothing other than the ark was kept in the Most Holy Place.
2. Because the ark, covered by the mercy seat, was God's throne, all the wood had to be covered with pure gold, to express His holiness and purity.
3. The carrying poles were always left in the rings on the sides of the ark so that it could be shown that God was always ready to travel wherever His people went. He would always be with them.
4. The ark was called the "ark of the testimony" because it contained the tables of the testimony – the two tablets of stone with the Ten Commandments inscribed on them.
5. The tables of stone witnessed to men and women what God requires of any who would wish to serve Him.

Chapter 18 – "The Mercy Seat"

PAGE 57

1. The Mercy Seat was constructed only from pure gold. No other material was used.

2. The only other item in the tabernacle also made solely from pure gold was the lampstand which stood in the Holy Place.
3. The cherubim Ezekiel saw had four faces. Most probably each of these faces looked in a different direction. The faces of the two cherubim on the mercy seat were directed to the top of the mercy seat.
4. Physically, there was nothing at all between the cherubim. But actually it was the place where the glory of God rested.
5. As the tabernacle had an all-important central part, so should our lives. If God is truly at the centre of all we do, we can become "a dwelling place of God in the Spirit" (Ephesians 2:22).

Chapter 19 – "Setting up the tabernacle"

PAGE 60

1. As the nucleus of the tabernacle, the ark and the mercy seat were the first things to be placed inside it when it was erected.
2. The tabernacle was a "sanctuary", something set aside for the worship of God. It needed to be dedicated and sanctified for this use. This was done when every part was specially anointed.
3. In Israel, kings and priests were anointed to separate and dedicate them for the work they were to do. In New Testament times, when the Gospel truth was being spread throughout the world, the apostles were also anointed by the power of God (see Acts 13:2).
4. Before Aaron was selected to be a priest, Melchizedek, who met Abraham as he returned from rescuing Lot and the inhabitants of Sodom, was "priest of the most high God" (Genesis 14:18).
5. Jesus is now High Priest for believers, and "he is able *for all time* to save those who draw near to God through him, since he always lives to make intercession for them" (Hebrews 7:25, RSV).

Chapter 20 – "The tabernacle on the move"

PAGE 63

1. Only the ark of the testimony had its blue cloth covering visible when the nation of Israel was moving to its next camping site. All the other items of furniture, except the laver, were covered finally with badgers' skins.
2. The blue cloth, as every other use of blue throughout the tabernacle, showed the holiness of God. The covering of skins showed that man can only associate with God on the basis of sacrifice.

3. The Kohathite family had a special responsibility for transporting the tabernacle whenever it was moved.
4. Items of furniture that had no carrying poles were placed on planks, so that the weight could be easily shared between two or more men, and so that the item itself did not need to be touched.
5. All the items specially covered by Aaron and his sons were holy. If the Kohathites touched them, the penalty was death.

All Bible Study shows, as has our consideration of the tabernacle, that God is holy, and His ways are far beyond the ways of man. Yet in His mercy, willing-hearted men and women can become associated with His righteousness through the Lord Jesus Christ.

CHAPTER 22

Moving on

ONE of the main purposes of this series of Study Guides is to encourage you to take a deeper interest in the things of God. We hope the outline of the tabernacle that has been provided will stimulate you to look elsewhere in the Bible, to expand on the themes introduced in this book.

Though there is nothing better than a good familiarity with the various books in the Bible to get the most out of further study, marginal references and a good Concordance are always useful. It could be that you are using a Bible without references. But, if you want to make your exploration of God's word the serious subject it should be, then be advised to obtain a Bible with good references. Many Bible Study aids are referenced to the King James Version, and a translation compatible with this is therefore helpful as your main version for study, complementing it with other versions which may aid the clarity of the message, or your understanding of it.

A Concordance is like a dictionary which lists all the occurrences in the Bible of any word you look up. It should also assist you in distinguishing between different words in the Hebrew and Greek (the original languages of the Old and New Testaments). *Young's Concordance* or *Strong's* are the best. These concordances often underpin online Bibles, and can be accessed from good Bible study programs.

Before you commence any further study, remember to start with a *prayer*. For the object is to get a closer understanding of God and His purpose, and to let Him speak to us through His word. Paul sums up why we should study the Bible:

> "All scripture is inspired by God, and profitable for teaching, for reproof, for correction, and for training in righteousness, that the man of God may be complete, equipped for every good work."
>
> (2 Timothy 3:16,17, RSV)

Some possible assignments

- Try to trace the history of the tabernacle. Find where it was erected when the nation of Israel finally reached the land God had promised them. Was the tabernacle the important centre of their worship once they were established in the land as it had been in the wilderness?
- The one important lesson taught by the tabernacle, that God wishes to dwell among

His people, was never fully understood by the nation of Israel. Look for the various ways they misapplied the instructions provided by Him when the tabernacle was in their midst.

- The importance of *the cherubim* in God's purpose is shown by their presence in the tabernacle. Look up all the references to cherubim in the rest of the Bible and try to learn more of what this beautiful idea can teach.
- A good knowledge of the tabernacle, and of the Law of Moses, is needed before the Letter to the Hebrews (in the New Testament) can be properly appreciated. As a first step, try reading Hebrews chapter 9 to see how some of the things you have already learned are used to show the uniqueness of Christ's redeeming work. Then try other parts of this letter to expand your understanding of how the Lord Jesus Christ fulfilled all the things the Law of Moses was unable to achieve.
- If you find the information in Hebrews interesting, go through the whole book, noting how often the principles established in the tabernacle are emphasised. Look for words like *holy place*, *sanctuary*, *incense*, etc.
- The tabernacle was only a part of God's provision through Moses to teach the Israelites about His purpose. You may like to study the work of the priests, or the offerings required from the people, or the various feasts kept each year.

CHAPTER 23

Further reading

THE following books are recommended for more detailed study of the tabernacle, and have been particularly helpful to the author of this Study Guide:

- *Law and Grace*, by W. F. Barling (The Christadelphian Office)
- *The Law of Moses*, by Robert Roberts (The Christadelphian Office)
- *The Letter to the Hebrews*, by John Carter (The Christadelphian Office)
- *Offerings, Feasts & Sanctuary*, by F. E. Mitchell (The Christadelphian Office)
- *"Let them make me a Sanctuary"*, (Christadelphian Scripture Study Service)
- *The tabernacle in the Wilderness*, by K. Cook (Logos Publications)
- *The tabernacle, the Priesthood and the Offerings*, by H. W. Soltau (available from The Christadelphian Office)
- *The Tabernacle of Israel*, by James Strong (available from the Christadelphian Office).

An excellent set of booklets covering basic doctrines is available from the Christadelphian Office, along with many other useful aids to study. Write or call for details.

Whatever you read, make sure it takes you *to* the Bible, not *away* from it!